MOBY-DICK

Ishmael's Mighty Book

MOBY-DICK

Ishmael's Mighty Book

Kerry McSweeney

TWAYNE PUBLISHERS • BOSTON
A Division of G.K. Hall & Co.

For Lucy and Kendra

MOBY DICK: ISHMAEL'S MIGHTY BOOK
Kerry McSweeney

Twayne's Masterwork Studies
No. 3

Copyright © 1986 by G.K. Hall & Co.
All Rights Reserved
Published by Twayne Publishers
A Division of G.K. Hall & Co.
70 Lincoln Street, Boston, Massachusetts 02111

Copyediting supervised by Lewis DeSimone
Designed and produced by Marne B. Sultz
Typeset in Sabon with Garamond Italic display by Compset, Inc.

Printed on permanent/durable acid-free paper
and bound in the United States of America

First Printing

Library of Congress Cataloging in Publication Data

McSweeney, Kerry, 1941–
   Moby-Dick: Ishmael's mighty book.

   (Twayne's masterwork studies; no. 3)
   Bibliography: p. 121
   Includes index.
   1. Melville, Herman, 1819–1891.   Moby-Dick.
I. Title. II. Series.
PS2384.M62M37 1986   813'.3   86-4839
ISBN 0-8057-7954-X
ISBN 0-8057-8002-5 (pbk)

Contents

Acknowledgments

My study assumes a reader who already has a reasonable knowledge of the text of *Moby-Dick*, and is intended to help him or her to a more fine-grained and comprehensive awareness of the work than can be provided in a lecture or seminar room. *Moby-Dick* has received an enormous amount of scholarly and critical attention over the last four decades, and I am much indebted to earlier commentators. I am particularly grateful to William David Allen, whose Queen's University doctoral dissertation on *Moby-Dick* I had the pleasure of supervising some ten years ago and who first started me thinking seriously about Melville's marvelous book. Adrienne Brown typed the manuscript and Peter Sabor was good enough to read and comment on it. The Berkshire Athenaeum kindly granted permission to use Rodney Dewey's 1861 photograph of Melville.

All quotations from *Moby-Dick* are from Charles Feidelson's edition (Indianapolis: Bobbs-Merrill, 1964). The sources of quotations from other works of Melville are identified in the notes. The Chronology I have supplied depends on Jay Leyda's *Melville Log* and Leon Howard's biography. The items in the Selected Bibliography are meant to supplement as well as to complement my text and to suggest something of the wide variety of the available commentary on *Moby-Dick*.

I am indebted as always to my wife, Susanne, for her advice, expert assistance, and good humor.

Quotations from Emily Dickinson are reprinted by permission of the publishers and the Trustees of Amherst College from *The Poems of Emily Dickinson,* edited by Thomas H. Johnson (Cambridge, Mass.: The Belknap Press of Harvard University Press), copyright 1951, © 1955, 1979, 1983 by the President and Fellows of Harvard College. Also reprinted by permission of Little, Brown and Company, Inc.

HERMAN MELVILLE
Photograph by Rodney Dewey
Courtesy of Berkshire Athenaeum

Chronology of Herman Melville's Life

1819   Herman Melville born in New York City on 1 August, third child (of eight) of Allan Melvill, a merchant, and Maria Gansevoort, daughter of General Peter Gansevoort of Albany, a hero of the American Revolution.

1825   Enters New York Male High School, which he attends for four years.

1829   Attends Columbia Grammar School, New York.

1830   Because of business failure, Allan Melvill and family move to Albany; attends Albany Academy from October 1830 to October 1831.

1832   Allan Melvill dies in January, in debt; goes to work as a clerk at the New York State Bank in Albany.

1834   Works for a time on his uncle Thomas's farm near Pittsfield, Massachusetts.

1835   Works in Albany as bookkeeper and clerk in his brother's fur business; attends Albany Classical School.

1836   Returns to Albany Academy in September; remains until following March.

1837   Brother's business fails; teaches in a district school near Pittsfield.

1838   Moves with family to Lansingburgh, near Albany; studies surveying and engineering at the Lansingburgh Academy.

1839   Two "Fragments from a Writing Desk" published pseudonymously in *Democratic Press and Lansingburgh Advertiser*. Sails from New York to Liverpool and back as crew member on the merchant ship *St. Lawrence*, spending five weeks in Liverpool. Teaches school in Greenbush, New York.

1840   Summer visit to Galena, Illinois; returns to New York City in the autumn and unsuccessfully looks for work.

1841   Sails from New Bedford, 3 January 1841, on the maiden voyage of the whaling ship *Acushnet,* bound for the South Seas.

1842   In July, after eighteen months on the *Acushnet,* deserts with Richard Tobias Greene at Nuku Hiva in the Marquesas. After a month in the Taipi valley, sails on the Australian whaling ship *Lucy Ann;* at Tahiti, is sent ashore with others as mutineer; escapes in October; explores Tahiti and Eimeo and works on a potato farm. Sails on the Nantucket whaling ship *Charles and Henry* in November.

1843   Discharged at Lahaina in the Hawaiian Islands in May; takes various jobs in Honolulu. Enlists in the United States Navy; sails in August aboard a frigate.

1844   Arrives in Boston in October, having been away nearly four years, and is discharged from the Navy. Returns to Lansingburgh.

1845   Works on a book based on his adventures in the Marquesas; it is rejected by an American publisher but accepted by John Murray in London.

1846   *Narrative of a Four Months' Residence among the Natives of a Valley of the Marquesas Islands* published in London in February; published the next month in New York, under the title *Typee: A Peep at Polynesian Life.*

1847   *Omoo: A Narrative of Adventures in the South Seas* published in London in late March and in New York in early May. In New York, Melville writes for the *Literary World,* edited by his friend Evert A. Duyckinck, and contributes satirical material to *Yankee Doodle.* On 4 August marries Elizabeth Shaw, daughter of Lemuel Shaw, Chief Justice of the Massachusetts Supreme Court. After a honeymoon in northern New England and Canada, the couple sets up housekeeping in New York.

1849   A son, Malcolm, born in February. *Mardi* published in London in March and in New York the following month. *Redburn: His First Voyage* published in London in September and in New York in November. Leaves in October on a trip to London (to visit publishers) and the continent; returns to America the following February.

1850   *White-Jacket; or, The World in a Man-of-War* published in London in January and New York in March. Begins work on a book based on his experiences on a whaling ship. Meets Nathaniel Hawthorne at a picnic near Pittsfield on 5 August; they become friends. "Hawthorne and His Mosses" published in the *Literary World*. Purchases a farm near Pittsfield in September and moves there with his family.

1851   Friendship with Hawthorne, who is also living in the Berkshires, continues to develop while Melville works hard on *Moby-Dick*, which is finished in July and published (under the title *The Whale*) in London in October. *Moby-Dick; or, The Whale* published in New York in November. A second son, Stanwix, born in October.

1852   *Pierre; or, The Ambiguities* published in New York in August and in London in November. Visits Hawthorne at Concord in December.

1853   A daughter, Elizabeth, born in May. Melville's family and friends concerned about his health. His wife's family concerned about her life with Melville. Begins writing tales and sketches for *Putnam's Monthly Magazine* and *Harper's New Monthly Magazine*.

1855   A second daughter, Frances, born in March. *Israel Potter: His Fifty Years of Exile* published in New York in early March (having been previously serialized in *Putnam's*).

1856   *The Piazza Tales*, consisting of five of the *Putnam's* pieces and a newly written title piece, published in New York in May. Sails for Glasgow in October on a therapeutic voyage; visits Hawthorne in Liverpool; then tours the Holy Land, Greece, and Italy; returns to New York the following May.

1857   *The Confidence-Man: His Masquerade* published in New York and London in April. First of three seasonal lecture tours; "Statues in Rome," "The South Seas," and "Travelling" are the successive subjects.

1860   Delivers his last lecture in February. Sails in May from New York around Cape Hope to San Francisco on a clipper ship as a guest of its captain, his brother Thomas; returns via Panama, arriving in New York in November.

1861   Travels to Washington to attempt to secure a consular appointment. Lemuel Shaw dies.

1863   Leaves Pittsfield permanently in October, moving to a house at 104 East 26th Street in New York.

1864   Visits his cousin Colonel Henry Gansevoort in an army camp on the Virginia front.

1866   Some Civil War poems published in *Harper's*. A collection of poems, *Battle-Pieces and Aspects of the War,* published in August. Appointed an inspector of customs at the port of New York.

1867   His son Malcolm dies of a self-inflicted bullet wound.

1872   Melville's mother dies, aged 81.

1876   The book-length *Clarel: A Poem and Pilgrimage in the Holy Land* published (at his uncle's expense) in early June.

1878   Melville's wife receives a substantial inheritance from her aunt.

1885   Resigns position as customs inspector.

1886   Son Stanwix dies in San Francisco after a long illness.

1888   Sails to Bermuda in February, his last voyage. *John Marr and Other Sailors with Some Sea Pieces* privately printed in an edition of twenty-five copies.

1891   *Timoleon and Other Ventures in Minor Verse* privately printed in May in an edition of twenty-five copies. Continues to revise *Billy Budd, Sailor,* published posthumously. Dies 28 September after two years of failing health. One obituary notice in the New York press, headlined "Death of a Once Popular Author,"observes that "probably, if the truth were known, even his own generation has long thought him dead, so quiet have been the later years of his life."

I: Historical Context

> The world,—this shadow of the soul, or *other me,*
> lies wide around. Its attractions are the keys which
> unlock my thoughts and make me acquainted with
> myself. I run eagerly into this resounding tumult.
>
> *Emerson, "The American Scholar"*

During the summer of 1850, Melville interrupted work on *Moby-Dick* to write an enthusiastic essay on his older contemporary Nathaniel Hawthorne, whose work he had just discovered. Among other things, "Hawthorne and His Mosses" contains predictions of the coming greatness of a native American literature. To "believe in Shakespeare's unapproachability" was an unworthy belief "for an American, a man who is bound to carry republican progressiveness into Literature, as well as into life." The "great mistake," even among "those Americans who look forward to the coming of a great literary genius among us," was to assume that "he will come in the costume of Queen Elizabeth's day, be a writer of dramas founded upon old English history, or the tales of Boccaccio. Whereas great geniuses are parts of the times; they themselves are the times, and possess a correspondent coloring." It is incorrect to say that "the world is getting gray and grizzled now, and has lost that fresh charm which she wore of old, and by virtue of which the great poets of past times made themselves what we esteem them to be. Not so. The world is as young today as when it was created."[1]

Melville was hardly alone in anticipating the imminent emergence of a distinctive national literature. His essay was a contribution to a long-running debate on the nature of an as yet unwritten American literature. On one side of the debate, as Larzer Ziff explains, "were those who believed that American literature would best develop organically from its English roots and that the task of American literary men was to treat American themes in

1

such a way as to link them with the best that had been said and thought in the Old World. Americans spoke the language of Shakespeare and this bound them to an essentially British outlook, as Edward Everett, for one, maintained."[2] On the other side were advocates like Ralph Waldo Emerson, who in 1836 wondered why Americans should not enjoy "an original relation to the universe. Why should not we have a poetry and philosophy of insight and not of tradition? . . . Why should we grope among the dry bones of the past, or put the living generation into masquerade out of its faded wardrobe? . . . There are new lands, new men, new thoughts."[3] A decade later, it was still not clear that such a literature had come into being. In 1846, the same year that Melville's first book was published, Margaret Fuller began an article entitled "American Literature" by remarking that "some thinkers may object to this essay, that we are about to write of that which has as yet no existence. For it does not follow because many books are written by persons born in America that there exists an American literature."[4] Ten years after that, however, there could be no doubt that a native literature of marked originality had come into being. The first three of Hawthorne's four novels—including *The Scarlet Letter,* his masterpiece—were published between 1850 and 1852; Thoreau's *Walden* appeared in 1854; and the first edition of Whitman's *Leaves of Grass* came out in 1855, four years after the publication of *Moby-Dick.*

Distinctive thematic features of *Moby-Dick,* as of *Walden* and the 1855 *Leaves of Grass,* reflect the confident and expanding American society of the period. One is the emphasis on self-reliance, on firsthand experiential knowledge and on establishing, in Emerson's prescient phrase, "an original relation to the universe." At the beginning of his *Song of Myself,* Whitman promises the reader who will "stop this day and night with me" that "you shall possess the good of the earth and sun. . . . You shall no longer take things at second or third hand . . . nor look through the eyes of the dead . . . nor feed on the spectres in books."[5] In the "What I Lived For" chapter of *Walden* Thoreau explains that "I went to the woods because I wished to live deliberately, to front only the essential facts of life. . . . I wanted to live deep and suck out all the marrow of life . . . to drive life into a corner, and . . . if it proved to be mean, why then to get the whole and genuine meanness of it . . . or if it were sublime, to know it by experience." And when at the end of *Walden* Thoreau explains that he left the woods after two years because he felt he had several more lives to live, the image that he uses recalls Ishmael's itch to get to sea in the first chapter of *Moby-Dick:* "I did not wish," says Thoreau, "to take a cabin passage, but rather to go before the mast and on the deck of the world."[6]

At the entrepreneurial level, self-reliance leads to rugged individualism, the commercial exploitation of frontiers, and ultimately, at the level of national mythology, to the notion of America's Manifest Destiny. A good example of the commercial aggressiveness of American society was its sperm whale fishery. In chapter 25, Ishmael informs the reader that the American whaling industry of the time employed around eighteen thousand men in upwards of seven hundred ships and annually imported "into our harbours a well reaped harvest of $7,000,000."[7] This "high and mighty business of whaling," as Ishmael calls it in the same chapter, was not only perilously testing; it also involved collateral activities "remarkable in themselves, and . . . momentous in their sequential issues." The whaling ship, for example, was "the pioneer" in discovering some of "the remotest and least known parts of the earth." It was all very well to celebrate European captains of exploring expeditions like George Vancouver, James Cook, and Adam Johann von Krusenstern, but Ishmael insists that "scores of anonymous Captains have sailed out of Nantucket, that were as great, and greater."

Some commentators argue that *Moby-Dick* not only describes one example of nineteenth-century America's commercial expansion, but also offers a prophetic criticism of unbridled industrialization and predatory capitalism. In this view, the *Pequod* becomes "a mobile replica of a technically advanced, complex society" and the "The Try-Works" chapter is seen to "form a composite image of industrial technology in the Age of Steam."[8] And Ahab becomes a type of robber baron.[9] In this view, it is not for nothing that the captain of the *Pequod* uses the railroad—the sine qua non of nineteenth-century industrialism and commercial expansion—as an image of his inflexible will: "The path to my fixed purpose is laid with iron rails, whereon my soul is grooved to run. Over unsounded gorges, through the rifled hearts of mountains, under torrents' beds, unerringly I rush! Naught's an obstacle, naught's an angle to the iron way!" (chap. 38).

A third characteristically American aspect of *Moby-Dick* is its democratic assumptions and rhetoric. In the debate over a national literature some took the view bluntly expressed by old John Quincy Adams "that literature was, and in its nature must always be, aristocratic; that democracy of numbers and literature were self-contradictory."[10] But others held that a distinctly American literature would necessarily be democratic, would in Emerson's words "embrace the common [and] explore and sit at the feet of the familiar, the low."[11] It was even thought in some circles that non-American literature could be politically contaminating. As the *Democratic Review,* organ of the Young America group of literary nationalists, observed in its first number in 1837: "our 'better educated classes' drink in an anti-democratic habit of feeling and thinking from the . . . fountain of the literature of England."[12] For some, the unwholesome British spring even included Shakespeare who, Whitman argued, "belongs essentially to the buried past." His work rests upon "conditions, standards, politics, sociologies, ranges of belief" that are obsolete, and as "authoritative types" his works pertain to America "just about as much as the persons and institutes they depict."[13]

Melville's response to Shakespeare, while positive and liberating, was not untouched by these views. In an 1849 letter he exclaimed: "I would to God that Shakespeare had lived later, & promenaded in Broadway," cryptically adding that had he done so "the muzzle which all men wore on their souls in the Elizabethan day, might not have intercepted [his] full articulations. . . . The Declaration of Independence makes a difference."[14] This same democratic self-consciousness can be seen in Ishmael. At the end of chapter 33 he no sooner calls himself a "tragic dramatist" than he goes on to point out that his principal subject is not an emperor or king but "a poor old whale-hunter . . . therefore, all outward majestical trappings and housings are denied me." In a democratic age Ahab's greatness and grandeur must be supplied by natural images and associations, must be "plucked at from the skies, and dived for in the deep, and featured in the unbodied air!" And in chapter 26 Ishmael insists that the dignity he speaks of in connection with the *Pequod*'s crew "is not the dignity of kings and robes, [but] that democratic dignity which, on all hands, radiates without end from God." This "just Spirit of Equality," this "great democratic God," spreads "one royal mantle of humanity over all my kind!"

While there are distinctively American features and emphases in *Moby-Dick*, Melville's novel must also be placed in the larger context of the literature and thought of the Romantic period and, like Emerson's essays, *Walden,* and *Leaves of Grass,* be seen as part of the transatlantic flowering of the great imaginative germination begun more than fifty years earlier in England and Germany.[15] The fundamental feature of Romantic thought is the epistemological distinction, taken over from German idealist philosophy, between the understanding and the Reason. The former mental faculty was essentially passive, a tabula rasa on which came to be inscribed information ultimately derived solely from sense experience. Such empirical knowledge was strictly limited by space and time and could only supply knowledge of the appearances of things, not of things in themselves. Such knowledge could be objective, scientific, and useful; it could, for example, furnish quadrants, maps, and tempered steel. But it could never tell one anything about things in themselves or about noumenal (rather than phenomenal) objects of thought; the existence of God, an afterlife, or the soul could never be established through empirical understanding.

Noumenal knowledge was supplied by the intuitive faculty of the capital-R Reason, the operation of which was not dependent on the objects of sense experience. This faculty tended to regard, in Emerson's phrase, "every natural fact [as] a symbol of some spiritual fact."[16] It was this active faculty that gave the objects of sense experience meaning and value, and made them essentially alive rather than fixed and dead. As Ishmael insists: "some certain significance lurks in all things, else all things are little worth, and the

round world itself but an empty cipher, except to sell by the cart-
load, or as they do hills about Boston, to fill up some morass in
the Milky Way" (chap. 99). Reason was also the faculty of spiritual
or imaginative insight that made possible those sublime experiences in which a person's sense of a limited and mortal individual
identity was dissolved in an expanded consciousness and replaced
by an ecstatic sense of oneness with the universe. In such experiences, in Emerson's memorable description: "all mean egotism van-
ishes. I become a transparent eye-ball; I am nothing; I see all; the
currents of the Universal Being circulate through me; I am part or
particle of God."[17] The generic name that Emerson's friend Carlyle
gave to such experiences and their radiant afterglow—"natural
supernaturalism"[18]—adumbrates a key aspect of the Romantic
preoccupation with transporting moments: they seemed to give
an assurance that in the nineteenth century could no longer be re-
liably supplied by traditional Christian beliefs, of immortality and
of a larger existence beyond the boundaries of the passive
understanding.

In Emerson, Thoreau, and the early Whitman, the assertions
based on these Romantic assumptions are breathtakingly positive
and optimistic. At the beginning of *Nature,* for example, Emerson
is assured that "undoubtedly we have no questions to ask which
are unanswerable" and proclaims his confident trust that "what-
ever curiosity the order of things has awakened in our minds, the
order of things can satisfy."[19] And in the rhapsodic climax of *Walden* Thoreau celebrates the spiritual facts corresponding to the natural facts of the return of spring: "In a pleasant spring morning all
men's sins are forgiven. . . . Through our own recovered innocence
we discern the innocence of our neighbors. . . . There needs no
stronger proof of immortality. All things must live in such a
light."[20] Such ravishing assertions, however, are not the defining
characteristic of Romantic thought, though they are an essential
constituent. One is a Romantic if one is committed to an *in-out*
rather than pre-Romantic *up-down* schema.[21] Committed, that is,
to the belief that meaning, significance, and/or revelation, if they
are to be found anywhere, are out there in the visible world, and
do not descend from above. In M. H. Abrams's terms, Romantics

sought to take "traditional concepts, schemes, and values which had been based on the relation of the Creator to his creatures and creation, [and] reformulate them within the prevailing two-term system of subject and object, ego and non-ego, the human mind or consciousness and its transactions with nature."[22] Heaven or immortality becomes not a transcendent realm up there, but the state of being vibrantly united to the visible world. Nor is hell down there; it is rather one's self when cut off from any life-giving contact with the world of nature.

Melville is not anti-Romantic, but he is a caustic analyst of a facile and self-deluding Romanticism that does not take full and mature account of human experience. At the end of a letter to Hawthorne he quotes Goethe's saying "'*Live in the all.*' That is to say, your separate identity is but a wretched one,—good; but get out of yourself, spread and expand yourself, and bring to yourself the tinglings of life that are felt in the flowers and the woods, that are felt in the planets Saturn and Venus, and the Fixed Stars. What nonsense." Melville wonders what good this advice could be to "a fellow with a raging toothache." He goes on to say, however, that "there is some truth" in Goethe's *all* feeling and that he has himself experienced such moments. "But what plays the mischief with the truth is that men will insist upon the universal application of a temporary feeling or opinion."[23] In *Moby-Dick*, both central characters, Ishmael and Ahab, are Romantic questers committed to the search for the spiritual facts symbolized by natural facts. As the latter exclaims at the end of chapter 70: "O Nature, and O soul of man! how far beyond all utterance are your linked analogies." But the natural facts that compel their deepest attention are not the flora and fauna of Walden Pond or vernal leaves of grass. More than anything else it is the monstrous white whale that rivets them and that Ishmael insists must be fully taken into account in any reading of the universe: "For unless you own [acknowledge] the whale, you are but a provincial and sentimentalist in Truth" (chap. 76).

One important source of the darkness of Melville's Romantic vision was the Calvinistic Christianity of his childhood, which was similar to the New England Puritan inheritance that drew him to the works of Hawthorne. It was "this great power of blackness" in Hawthorne's tales "that so fixes and fascinates me," Melville wrote in "Hawthorne and His Mosses." He explained that this power "derives its force from its appeals to that Calvinistic sense of Innate Depravity and Original Sin, from whose visitations, in some shape or other, no deeply thinking mind is always and wholly free."[24] Melville became intimate with Hawthorne, his neighbor in the Berkshires, during the crucial months of late 1850 and early 1851 when he was finishing *Moby-Dick* (though Hawthorne's congenital reserve made the intimacy unilateral). It was to Hawthorne that Melville was to dedicate *Moby-Dick* and to express "a sense of unspeakable security . . . on account of your having understood the book. I have written a wicked book, and feel spotless as the lamb."[25] But while Hawthorne's proximity undoubtedly exerted an atmospheric influence on *Moby-Dick,* a number of other authors had a more specific influence. One of them was Thomas Carlyle, whose *Sartor Resartus,* read by Melville in 1850, contains the same mixture of Romantic and Calvinist temperaments found in *Moby-Dick* and, like Melville's book, employs an uncertain, self-conscious narrator who is energetically, zanily, and sometimes desperately attempting to discover coherence and meaning in the material on which he is working. Another influence was the Book of Job, that profound exploration of the problem of evil and suffering in human experience. A third was an English translation of Pierre Bayle's *Dictionnaire historique et critique,* bought in 1849, which supplied Melville, a metaphysically curious autodidact, with a wealth of philosophical history, theological argument, and curious speculation.[26] These influences, and a number of others, all make their presence felt in *Moby-Dick.* But the most dominant presence is that of Shakespeare, whom Melville thought a native American genius could rival, and who had given voice through the mouths of his "dark characters" (Hamlet, Timon, Lear, Iago) to his sense of the power of blackness, of those "things which we feel to be so terrifically true that it were all but madness for any good man, in his own proper character, to utter, or even hint of them."[27]

II: A Mighty Book

It is our best book.

Robert Lowell, "Epics"

In chapter 104 of *Moby-Dick*, Ishmael, the novel's first-person narrator, speaks of "the virtue of a large and liberal theme! We expand to its bulk. To produce a mighty book, you must choose a mighty theme. No great and enduring volume can ever be written on the flea, though many there be who have tried it." Strictly speaking, Ishmael was referring to his book's principal subject—whales—rather than to its theme. The mighty theme of *Moby-Dick* is the quest for what Ishmael calls "the ungraspable phantom of life" (chap. 1), "that demon phantom that, some time or other, swims before all human hearts" (chap. 52), the predominant embodiment of which in the novel is Moby Dick itself, that "grand hooded phantom, like a snow hill in the air" (chap. 1). This quest involves profound explorations of fundamental epistemological, psychological, and metaphysical questions: what if anything can be known with certainty? can meaning or significance be found in the world outside the self or even in personal experience? do human beings have free will or free choice and if not who or what shapes human destiny? what is "the secret of our paternity" (chap. 114) that makes us what we are? is there an afterlife or at least something beyond the visible world other than "inscrutable malice" (chap. 36) or a blank whiteness signifying only "the heartless voids and immensities of the universe"? is there an abiding alternative to the suicidal impulses or self-destructive obsessions that come in the wake of "the knowledge of the demonism of the world" (chap. 42)? how adequate are Christian beliefs in the face of such knowledge? and what is the status of the transporting but fragile experiences of friendship and love, and of oneness with the visible world?

Moby-Dick was published in 1851. Melville had been thinking of Emerson when he said in 1849 that "I love all men who *dive*. Any fish can swim near the surface, but it takes a great whale to go down stairs five miles or more; & if he don't attain the bottom, why, all the lead in Galena can't fashion the plumet that will."[28] And in the following year it was Shakespeare's greatness he was trying to define when he spoke of "those deep far-away things in him; those occasional flashings-forth of the intuitive Truth in him; those sharp quick probings at the very axis of reality."[29] These descriptions apply equally well to the author of *Moby-Dick* and in both cases it is hard not to think that Melville was giving indirect expression to his own vast ambition to write a mighty book about a great whale. Of course, mighty thematic content does not of itself make a literary work compelling, let alone great. Much of this critical study will be concerned with the *ways* in which Melville has articulated, shaped, and presented his probings at the axis of reality. For the moment one may simply say that the comprehensive vision of *Moby-Dick* is equaled by the originality and force of its execution. All of Melville's great gifts of language, invention, psychological analysis, speculative agility, and narrative power are fused to make *Moby-Dick* (to borrow another phrase of Ishmael's concerning his subject) "strike the imagination with unwonted [unaccustomed] power" (chap. 41). Even where Melville is simply recording "his sheer apprehension of the world," as D. H. Lawrence remarked, "he is wonderful: his book commands a stillness in the soul, an awe."[30]

Moby-Dick is unquestionably one of the masterpieces of nineteenth-century prose fiction in English. That century was the great age of the realistic novel, of which George Eliot's *Middlemarch: A Study of Provincial Life* is an exemplary text. But compared with *Moby-Dick,* Eliot's novel, despite its thematic richness and intellectual range, seems provincial not only in its subject matter but also in its assumptions that private life is shaped and conditioned by society and that the fundamental questions of human existence center on egotism and its antidotes. As the narrator of *Middlemarch* was perfectly aware, it inevitably follows from such postulates that in the modern world epic grandeur dwindles to the "home-epic" of marriage and its prelude, and tragedy becomes reduced to a matter of vocational frustration.[31] In its way, *Moby-Dick* is as committed to circumstantial realism as *Middlemarch*. Melville's narrator is at pains to establish "in all respects the reasonableness of the whole story of the White Whale, more especially the catastrophe"; "the plain facts" must be made known to the reader lest the narrative seem simply "a monstrous fable, or still worse and more detestable, a hideous and intolerable allegory" (chap. 45). But while *Middlemarch* hugs the shore of the known and the normal, *Moby-Dick* ventures into previously uncharted fictional waters and in so doing revitalizes epic and tragic forms in ways that add immeasurably to the resonance of the work.

T. E. Lawrence once told a correspondent that he had "collected a shelf of 'Titanic' books (those distinguished by greatness of spirit, 'sublimity' as Longinus would call it)." The books were *Moby-Dick*, Dostoevsky's *The Brothers Karamazov*, and Nietzsche's *Thus Spoke Zarathustra*. In a subsequent letter Lawrence added to his list of "the world's big books" Tolstoy's *War and Peace*, Rabelais's *Gargantua and Pantagruel*, and Cervantes's *Don Quixote*.[32] In several ways these works are more appropriate bedfellows for *Moby-Dick* than any grouping of prose fictions written in English. There are, however, significant differences between Melville's novel and the two other nineteenth-century novels in Lawrence's list. Unlike *War and Peace* and *The Brothers Karamazov*, Melville's book was not widely read, let alone recognized as a masterpiece, in its own century. It was not until the 1920s that its magnitude began to be generally acknowledged. The reasons for this are the formal originality of the novel and the modernity of its content. In form *Moby-Dick* is a boldly experimental work that anticipates some of the central techniques and devices of modernist and postmodernist prose fiction. The novel is a self-conscious, reflexive fiction in which the creative difficulties of the narrator are an overt concern. The novel ignores and/or subverts dominant nineteenth-century novelistic conventions and the assumptions that underlie them, and freely uses other conventions and genres in order to bring its deeper concerns into fuller focus.[33]

As George Steiner has done in his *Tolstoy or Dostoevsky: An*

Essay in the Old Criticism, one could speak of the greatness of *Moby-Dick* in terms of "a perfect accord between theme and mode of treatment."[34] But it is perhaps better to speak in a more contemporary critical idiom of the novel's greatness being indicated by the plurality of interpretative possibilities to which the indeterminacy of the text gives rise.[35] Such an approach calls more attention to the essentially problematic vision of *Moby-Dick,* which raises fundamental questions but offers no answers that are not equivocal and partial, and some answers that approach the nihilistic. In *Moby-Dick* the quest for that "demon phantom" seems inevitably to either "lead us on in barren mazes or midway leave us whelmed" (chap. 52).

Finally, no sketch of the importance or greatness of *Moby-Dick* would be complete that did not recognize its preeminent position in American literature. Of all the works produced during the mid-nineteenth-century creative flowering that has been called the American Renaissance, it is unquestionably the greatest single text. In the larger context of all American literature, *Moby-Dick* more than any other work deserves the oft-invoked but doubtfully useful title of "the great American novel." And, as Robert Lowell has insisted, Melville's book is "our epic, a New England epic": "*Moby-Dick* is fiction, not history—beside James or Dickens, how thin and few its characters, how heroic and barbarous its adventure. As a librettist once said to me, 'Not the faintest whisper of a female voice.' Often magnificent rhythms and a larger vocabulary make it equal to the great metrical poems. Parts, of course, are not even prose, but collages of encyclopedic clippings on cetology. It is our best book. It tells us not to break our necks on a brick wall. Yet what sticks in mind is the Homeric prowess of the extinct whaleman, gone before his prey."[36]

III: Composition and Reception

> But it is better to fail in originality than to succeed in imitation. He who has never failed somewhere, that man can not be great.
>
> *Melville, "Hawthorne and His Mosses"*

The qualities that make *Moby-Dick* a mighty book are the very ones that assured it would not find a wide audience in its own day. Melville was himself keenly aware of the difficulties of articulating his vision through the medium of prose fiction and of doing so in a way that would engage the attention of his contemporaries. He returns to the subject more than once in the extraordinary series of letters written to Hawthorne during the composition of *Moby-Dick*. Melville's deepest concern was with "visable truth," that is, with "the apprehension of the absolute condition of present things as they strike the eye of the man who fears them not, though they do their worst to him." But such a preoccupation was hardly prudent for someone with a family to support: "Try to get a living by the Truth—and go to the Soup Societies. . . . Truth is ridiculous to men." How could someone with such an interest influence his native land: America and "nearly all its affairs [were] governed by sturdy backwoodsmen—noble fellows enough, but not at all literary, & who care not a fig for any authors except those who write those most saleable of all books nowadays—ie—the newspapers, & magazines." What was the point, Melville asked in a dispirited moment, of his concentrating his energies on finishing something "so short-lived as a modern book? Though I wrote the Gospels in this century, I should die in the gutter." What he felt "most moved to write, that is banned,—it will not pay. Yet, altogether, write the *other* way I cannot. So the product is a final hash, and all my books are botches."[37]

Moby-Dick was Melville's sixth book, *Typee* (1846) and *Omoo* (1847), his first two, had been commercially successful. But these were straightforward documentary narratives closely based on his experiences in the South Pacific during the early 1840s, and in them his intention had been solely to "speak the unvarnished truth"—that is, to give faithful firsthand accounts of his adventures. *Typee* was "simply a record" of his residence among the natives of a valley of the Marquesas, "interspersed with accounts of the islanders, and occasional reflections naturally connected with the subject." And in the preface to *Omoo*, Melville even more strongly insisted that his book was strictly reportorial: "if reflections are occasionally indulged in, they are spontaneous, and such as would, very probably, suggest themselves to the most casual observer."[38]

When Melville began work on his third book, his apparent intention was to produce another documentary narrative based on his maritime experiences. But during the composition of *Mardi* (published in 1849) his intentions began to change. Melville had come to feel, he wrote to his British publisher, an "incurable distaste" for a "narrative of *facts*." He felt "irked, cramped & fettered by plodding along with dull common places," and longed "to plume [his] pinions for a flight."[39] Melville had clearly begun to sense that the travel-narrative mode offered insufficient opportunity for self-expression and intellectual speculation. As a result he attempted in midstream to change *Mardi* from a documentary into a romance, from a work devoted to "unvarnished truth" to one taking "visable truth" as its subject. The result was a frequently tedious hodgepodge, longer than *Typee* and *Omoo* combined, that understandably met with less critical and commercial success than either of its predecessors. Melville was chastened by his experience with *Mardi* and for his next two books, *Redburn* (1849) and *White-Jacket* (1850), he returned to the mode of straightforward narrative based on his experiences at sea. (The former made use of his time aboard the merchant ship on which he sailed from New York to Liverpool and back in 1839; the latter, of his time as an ordinary seaman on a United States Navy ship in 1843–44.) But from either of these books, Melville insisted, "no reputation that is gratifying to me can possibly be achieved. . . . They are two *jobs*, which I have done for money—being forced to it, as other men are to sawing wood." He had "felt obliged to refrain from writing the kind of book I would wish to." His concern for their "'success' (as it is called) springs from my pocket, & not from my heart. So far as I am individually concerned, & independent of my pocket, it is my earnest desire to write those sort of books which are said to 'fail'."[40]

This was Melville's state of mind as he began to think about the subject of his sixth book, in which he was ultimately to try to write a book that would not be simply a sea narrative based on personal experience but would also forcefully convey his sense of "visable truth." As he began work on *Moby-Dick*, however, Melville seemed to have had little inkling of what the book would become. In June 1850 he described to his British publisher the work that he anticipated finishing by the coming autumn. It was to be "a romance of adventure, founded upon certain wild legends in the Southern Sperm Whale Fisheries, and illustrated by the author's own personal experience."[41] (In 1841–42 Melville had spent eighteen months on an American whaling ship, the *Acushnet;* it was the one episode from his years at sea that he had not yet used in his books.) The prediction that *Moby-Dick* would be finished in a few months turned out to be wrong. The Melvilles moved from New York to the Berkshires for the summer of 1850. It was there that he read Hawthorne's tales for the first time and there, at a picnic near Pittsfield on 5 August, that he first met their author. Later that month, the *Literary World* published "Hawthorne and His Mosses," in which Melville, who had taken in a great deal of sail in his two previous books, confidently proclaimed that "you must have plenty of sea-room to tell the Truth in" and that "failure is the true test of greatness."[42] Clearly the shape and scale of *Moby-Dick* changed greatly during the pivotal summer of 1850. Far from finishing the book in a short time Melville worked steadily at it during the autumn and winter of that year and during the following spring and summer.

Can the stages of the composition of *Moby-Dick* be detected in the finished work? Up to a point, the answer is yes. One may distinguish two successive periods of composition and three stages in the gestation of the work. But to do so is not to suggest that there

are what used to be called "two *Moby-Dicks*" (two separately con-
ceived stories imperfectly conflated) or that the novel can be sep-
arated into discrete chunks. Such theories, as Robert Midler has
persuasively argued, do not withstand close examination.[43] In the
following chapters I shall be discussing in detail how *Moby-Dick*
is, on its own terms, a cohesive and seamless work: the account of
a self-conscious, retrospective narrator called Ishmael, who struggles to make sense of the experiences he shared, and the events he
witnessed, when he sailed on board the *Pequod* "some years ago"
(chap. 1).

The first stage of composition (from February to August 1850)
consists of chapters 1–22—from "Call me Ishmael" to the sailing
of the *Pequod* on Christmas day. One can confidently infer from
these chapters that Melville had begun to write a book in the pat-
tern of all his previous works save *Mardi:* "a mingling of personal
experience with exposition of an interesting milieu or way of life
connected with the sea, the whole 'cooked up' in a fanciful, romantic manner."[44] The second stage was written in the latter part
of 1850; it consists of chapters 60–92, which are primarily devoted
to the subject of whales and whaling, and probably includes the
other cetological chapters as well. To expand the bulk of his book,
and to give his narrative authenticity, Melville relied chiefly on four
published sources: Beale's *Natural History of the Sperm Whale* (his
primary source), Bennett's *A Whaling Voyage round the Globe,
from the Year 1833 to 1836,* Scoresby's classic *Account of the Arctic Regions with a History and Description of the Northern Whale
Fishery,* and Cheever's *The Whale and His Captors.*

The third stage in the composition includes chapter 26–42 (mi-
nus 35) and chapters 106 to the end, most of which were probably
written between early 1851 and the end of the following summer.
These chapters, one may say, grew from the "germinous seeds" that
Melville's reading of Hawthorne had "dropped . . . into my soul"
during the summer of 1850.[45] As we have seen, Hawthorne quick-
ened Melville's interest in the power of blackness, in Shakespeare,
and in writing an original and vastly ambitious American book.
The patent function of chapters 23–28 is to raise *Moby-Dick* from
a straightforward whaling narrative into an epic tragedy and to

find an appropriate rhetorical register for so daring a promotion. In chapter 23 ("The Lee Shore"), "the tall, new-landed mariner" named Bulkington, previously introduced in chapter 3, makes his second and final appearance in *Moby-Dick*. Presumably slated to play a larger role in the whaling narrative Melville had begun writing, Bulkington becomes vestigial after the author's discovery of the larger potentialities of his material. In his "apotheosis" in this chapter, Bulkington becomes a type of deep-thinking quester and heroic adventurer (a prefiguration of the as yet unintroduced Ahab), for whom it is better "to perish in that howling infinite, than be ingloriously dashed upon the lee, even if that were safety!" In the same way, chapter 36 ("The Quarter-Deck") and chapter 41 ("Moby Dick") are designed to raise Ahab to the stature of a tragic hero at the center of the book's dramatic action. Throughout this stage of composition the influence of Shakespearean tragedy is constantly felt—in the soliloquies and stage directions, in the rhythms of the prose, in echoes, allusions and derivations of character and incident, and in those "short, quick probings," as Melville called them, "at the very axis of reality."

Moby-Dick was finally published in New York on 14 November 1851 (for copyright reasons the British edition had appeared the previous month). Reviews in newspapers and periodicals on both sides of the Atlantic were numerous and on the whole may be described as mixed. No one found the novel dull and there was "a marked tendency for reviewers to indulge in extremes of praise or censure, sometimes both in the same article."[46] Almost everyone grappled with the problem of generic classification. "This is an odd book, professing to be a novel," one reviewer asserted: "wantonly eccentric, outrageously bombastic; in places charmingly and vividly descriptive";[47] another called it "a salmagundi of fact, fiction and philosophy"; for a third, the book was "an intellectual chowder of romance, philosophy, natural history, fine writing, good feeling, bad sayings."[48]

While the immediate critical reaction to *Moby-Dick* was equivocal and not unencouraging, the delayed popular reaction was decidedly negative. The sales record of the book in America shows that Melville failed to find the wide audience he desired. Only

2,500 copies of *Moby-Dick* were sold in its first five years, and fewer than 3,000 in its first twenty. (By comparison, *The Scarlet Letter*, during similar periods, sold 10,800 and 25,000 copies.)[49] One reason was that novel sales reflected the tastes of a genteel and predominantly female fiction-reading public, to which *Moby-Dick* had very little to offer. That Melville was perfectly aware of this is indicated by the letter he wrote to a female friend shortly before his book's publication. He advised her not to buy, and not even to read, *Moby-Dick*, "because it is by no means the sort of book for you. It is not a piece of fine feminine Spitalfields silk—but is of the horrible texture of a fabric that should be woven of ships' cables & hawsers. A Polar wind blows through it, & birds of prey hover over it. Warn all gentle fastidious people from so much as peeping into the book."[50]

Foreknowledge, however, is no antidote for bitter disappointment and intense frustration. The indirect expression of these emotions in Melville's next book, *Pierre; or, the Ambiguities* (1852), was one of the reasons for that peculiar novel's disastrous critical reception and extremely poor sales. Melville continued to attempt to make a living as a writer for several more years, but his reputation never recovered from *Pierre*, and after *The Confidence-Man* (1857) he gave up trying to support himself with his pen. The next three decades were spent in literary obscurity, and at his death in 1891 *Moby-Dick*, like his other books, had almost entirely sunk from sight.

Between the 1890s and the 1920s *Moby-Dick* slowly gained some recognition and a certain readership. In 1907, for example, it was published in the popular Everyman's Library series and by the end of the next decade—vide Carl Van Doren's assessment of Melville in the *Cambridge History of American Literature* (1917)—it had become recognized as its author's greatest book. During the 1920s the Melville revival began in earnest and *Moby-Dick* came to be hailed not simply as Melville's greatest book but as one of the great works of world literature. In 1929 Van Wyck Brooks had found "strange lapses" in the work that suggested imperfect artistic control. But two years later, after a third reading, Brooks grasped the epic nature of *Moby-Dick* and from that generic recognition followed the realization of "how cunning is its craftsmanship throughout" and "with what deliberate art Melville has ensnared his readers . . . how carefully, with what prevision, he has built up the general scheme."[51] And in the panegyrical chapter on *Moby-Dick* in his 1929 book on Melville (the last of three biographical-critical studies published during the decade) Lewis Mumford identified the work as "poetic epic," nay as "a symphony" in which "every resource of language and thought [was] utilized to sustain and expand the grand theme" of a work that was "fundamentally, a parable on the mystery of evil and the accidental malice of the universe."[52] The rising curve of Melville's reputation leveled off somewhat during the 1930s, but by the end of that decade the reputation of *Moby-Dick* was firmly established not only among men of letters but also among academic critics. And in 1941 F. O. Matthiessen published his major assessment, *American Renaissance: Art and Expression in the Age of Emerson and Whitman*, which included a long and influential discussion of *Moby-Dick*, the point d'appui of which was Matthiessen's adaptation of T. S. Eliot's notion of the several levels of significance in the plays of Shakespeare.

The early 1950s saw the publication of some critical and scholarly works of the first importance to the study of *Moby-Dick*. Mansfield and Vincent's 1952 Hendricks House edition offered 264 pages of explanatory notes. Leon Howard's excellent *Herman Melville: A Biography* (1951) contained the salutary reminder of the need to consider the novel "in relation to the literary tradition of which it was a part—that is . . . against the background of works by other writers who were in [Melville's] mind at the time he planned and wrote" his book.[53] Newton Arvin's 1950 study of Melville in the American Men of Letters series contained a chapter on *Moby-Dick* that remains one of the best shorter accounts of the work. Arvin identified four planes of significance: the first was the literal, which made *Moby-Dick* "symbolist romance that it is, [draw] close at one pole to the bias of naturalism." On the oneiric or psychological plane, features of the text were shown to become dreamlike projections of "Melville's unconscious wishes and obscure inward contests"; on the moral level (for Arvin implicitly the most important), the alternative to Ahab's destructive egotism was not the soft option of Christianity, but "a strong intuition of human solidarity as a priceless good," of which affirmations Ishmael was "the narrative agent." Finally, there was the mythic plane, on which the narrative was seen to embody "some form of the conflict between human wishes and nonhuman forces," through which Melville expressed his obsession with "the spectacle of a natural and human scene in which the instinctive need for order and meaning seems mainly to be confronted by meaninglessness and disorder."[54]

A volume of centennial essays published in 1953 contained two remarkable papers: Henry A. Murray's "In Nomine Diaboli," and Walter E. Bezanson's "*Moby-Dick:* Work of Art." In the former, Murray described the psychological content of the novel in Freudian terms. Ahab was "captain of the culturally repressed dispositions of human nature, that part of the personality which psychoanalysts have termed the 'Id'." The White Whale was "the internal institution which is responsible for these repressions, namely the Freudian Superego." Moby Dick "received the projection of Captain Ahab's Presbyterian conscience, and so may be said to embody the Old Testament Calvinistic conception of an affrighting Deity and his strict commandments, the derivative puritan ethic of nineteenth-century America, and the society that defended this ethic." Starbuck, the first mate, stood "for the rational realistic Ego, which is overpowered by the fanatical compulsiveness of the Id and dispossessed of its normal regulating functions."[55] While Murray did not even once mention Ishmael, the narrator of *Moby-Dick* was at the center of Bezanson's groundbreaking discussion, which identified Ishmael as "the real center of meaning and the defining force of the novel." But Bezanson stressed that there were two Ishmaels: the first was the narrator of the novel, "the imagination through which all matters of the book pass." The other Ishmael was "the young man of whom, among others, narrator Ishmael tells us in his story." The "prime experience for the reader" of *Moby-Dick* was "the narrator's unfolding sensibility," one key aspect of which was "the persistent tendency . . . for facts, events, and images to become symbols." It was above all the imagination of the narrator that set and defined "the symbolic mode that pervades the entire book."[56]

In his *Symbolism and American Literature,* also published in 1953, Charles Feidelson offered corroborating testimony that Ishmael was the key constituent of *Moby-Dick.* Feidelson's concern was to identify "the really vital common denominator" of the classic American writers: "a devotion to the possibilities of symbolism." *Moby-Dick* was a prime example: its "apparent violation of narrative standpoint is really a natural consequence of the symbolic method. . . . He who would follow Ishmael must exert the symbolic imagination." The reason Ishmael's presence was necessary in the book was that "the symbolic nature of the action depends on its being perceived."[57] Feidelson's study was one of a number of important overviews of American literature published during the 1950s and early 1960s in which *Moby-Dick* was a central exhibit. Richard Chase's *The American Novel and its Tradition* (1957) and Leo Marx's *The Machine in the Garden: Technology and the Pastoral Ideal in America* (1964) are other examples. So is Leslie Fiedler's *Love and Death in the American Novel* (1960; revised 1966), whose subject is "the American experience as recorded in our classic fiction." This literature was "distinguished by the number of dangerous and disturbing books in its canon." One striking aspect of the record was "the failure of the American fictionalist to deal with adult heterosexual love and his consequent obsession with death, incest and innocent homosexuality." *Moby-Dick* could be read "as a love story, perhaps the greatest love story in our fiction, cast in the peculiar American form of innocent homosexuality."[58] From this perspective Fiedler brilliantly analyzed the flagrant overtones and the subtle undertones of the coming together of the white Ishmael and the dark Queequeg early in the book as well as the sexual jokes, allusions, and puns that run through the text.

Since the 1950s, criticism of *Moby-Dick* has proliferated at a seemingly exponential rate. Investigation of the novel, Harry Levin observed as early as 1958, "might almost be said to have taken the place of whaling among the industries of New England."[59] Much of this commentary reflects the preoccupations of the contemporary critical temperament, and not all of it is sufficiently disinterested or skillful to be genuinely useful. The greatest potential danger to readers and students of *Moby-Dick*, however, is not inferior critical discourse but the sheer amount of available commentary, good and less good alike. As Marius Bewley observed over twenty-five years ago, the result of reading "what any three or four critics say of *Moby-Dick* . . . is painfully indigestible, both in the mind and in the emotional response one brings to Melville. . . . Where the possibilities of exegesis are so vast, the result must inevitably be a loss of salience."[60] In what follows I have tried to keep in mind both this sobering reflection and the fact that many first-time readers of *Moby-Dick* find the experience boring. No amount of learning or interpretative skill can overcome this visceral response unless at the same time the critic is able to convey something of his own felt sense of the novel's greatness and living power.

IV: "Call Me Ishmael"

> Affliction cannot stay
> In Acres—Its Location
> Is Illocality.
>
> *Emily Dickinson*

Everyone knows the opening sentence of the first chapter of *Moby-Dick*. But what does it mean? Is the greeting friendly and open—a hearty waiving of genteel formalities in favor of an immediate first-name intimacy?—or does it rather indicate the speaker's reserve and his sense of estrangement from others? Is he really saying: never mind what my real name is, but think of me as an outcast like the biblical Ishmael of whom it was prophesied that "he will be a wild man; his hand will be against every man, and every man's hand against him" (Gen. 16:12)? The rest of the opening paragraph of "Loomings" is of little help in determining the meaning of its opening sentence. Ishmael explains that he feels the need to go to sea "whenever it is a damp, drizzly November in my soul," especially whenever what he calls his "hypos" get such an upper hand that he is prompted to violence—especially violence against himself. His going to sea, he says, "is my substitute for pistol and ball. With a philosophical flourish Cato throws himself upon his sword; I quietly take to the ship." Again the reader is faced with alternative possibilities. Is this talk of suicide the rhetorical flourish of a well-read, self-dramatizing young man for whose life one need not seriously fear? "For nowadays," as Ishmael himself observes in chapter 35, "the whale-fishery furnishes an asylum for many romantic, melancholy, and absent-minded young men, disgusted with the carking cares of earth, and seeking sentiment in tar and blubber." Or is Ishmael in earnest when he speaks of the boundlessness of the ocean as an alternative to self-destruction, as he certainly is later when he describes the "unimaginable, taking [alluring] terrors, and wonderful, new-life adventures" that

23

the ocean has for "the death-longing eyes" of men who "still have left in them some interior compunctions against suicide" (chap. 112)?

Ishmael wants to go to sea; but what leads him to a whaling ship? In the opening chapter of *Moby-Dick*, he speculates on why he chose this particular kind of ocean voyage and in so doing presents the reader with a third pair of alternatives. Does the explanation lie with "the invisible police officer of the Fates, who has the constant surveillance of me"; does his joining a whaling ship "doubtless" form part of "the grand programme of Providence that was drawn up a long time ago"? Ishmael seems at one point to have believed this providential explanation of his action; but he goes on to say that with hindsight he suspects a different explanation may be correct—one that involves not metaphysical but psychological causation. "Now that I recall all the circumstances," he says,"I think I can see a little into the springs and motives which . . . induced me to set about performing the part I did. . . . Chief among these motives was the overwhelming idea of the great whale itself."

But this retrospective insight does not definitively settle the question of the "cunning" source of Ishmael's action. And for the reader it points to yet another set of alternative possibilities, this time concerning the origin of Ishmael's "overwhelming idea of the great whale," of the "portentous and mysterious monster [that] roused all my curiosity." For Ishmael the great whale is an image of "the ungraspable phantom of life," which in the last sentence of "Loomings" is more particularly imaged as "one grand hooded phantom, like a snow hill in the air." The reference is, of course, to the great albino whale Moby Dick. But before coming to New Bedford and Nantucket Ishmael had been "wholly ignorant of the mysteries of whaling" (chap. 12). How then can he have had a vision of a snow-hill phantom prior to boarding the *Pequod*, on which he first hears about Moby Dick?

One might speculate that the reason is psychological, and ask if there is any phantom in Ishmael's past, in his pre-*Pequod* life, that might have become the ruling passion of his psyche. The perimeters of such speculation are sharply circumscribed; with one exception, the reader can glean from the text virtually no information about Ishmael's life prior to the time when, after four voyages as a merchant seaman, he took it into his head to go on a whaling voyage. The one exception, however, though it occupies only two paragraphs in chapter 4 ("The Counterpane"), is extremely interesting in connection both with Ishmael's inner life in particular and with the larger issues of supernatural causation versus natural or psychological causation that run through *Moby-Dick*. In the chapter Ishmael recalls how when he was a child his severe stepmother once sent him to bed in the early afternoon of the longest day of the year with instructions not to rise until the following dawn. Eventually he fell into a half-dreaming, half-wakeful state of consciousness—"whether it was a reality or a dream, I never could entirely settle"—in which suddenly "a supernatural hand seemed placed in mine. My arm hung over the counterpane, and the nameless, unimaginable, silent form or phantom, to which the hand belonged, seemed closely seated by my bedside." During this experience Ishmael lay "frozen with the most awful fears." Afterwards, "I lost myself in confounding attempts to explain the mystery. Nay to this very hour, I often puzzle myself with it."

The alternative explanation of the presence of a silent white phantom in Ishmael's consciousness is not psychological but narratorial. It could be thought an example of artistic license on the part of Ishmael, the retrospective narrator, who is recounting with the aid of hindsight his whaling experiences on the *Pequod* that took place "some years ago." This explanation not only illuminates the question of the source of Ishmael's image of a grand, snow-hill phantom; once the distinction is made between Ishmael the character and Ishmael the narrator considerable light is thrown on the other pairs of alternative possibilities in "Loomings."

This distinction is fundamentally important not only to the first chapter but to all of *Moby-Dick*, and before going further it is essential to be clear about the differences between the two Ishmaels. The most helpful commentator is Franz Stanzel in his *Narrative Situations in the Novel*. The terms Stanzel uses to distinguish Ishmael as character from Ishmael as narrator are "experiencing self" and "narrating self." The latter stands in a relationship of posteriority to the former. It is clear, for example, that Ishmael's wide knowledge of cetology was acquired only after he had been a sailor on the *Pequod* and that the many cetological chapters of *Moby-Dick* reflect the interests and knowledge of the narrator Ishmael, not of the character Ishmael. But there is nonetheless a "demonstrated identity" between the experiencing self and narrating self. Because of this continuum the point of view and center of orientation can shift back and forth between a close-up view and a more distanced perspective without violating the reader's "illusion expectancy." In chapter 61, when Ishmael says that "it was my turn to stand at the foremast-head . . . to and fro I idly swayed in what seemed an enchanted air" the reader is in no doubt that Ishmael the character is speaking even though the previous chapter had begun with Ishmael the narrator explaining that "I have here to speak of the magical, sometimes horrible whale-line."

Another important point Stanzel makes is that since the narrative distance is greater than the duration of the narrated matter, the narrating self knows how the narrative will end. When he sails on the *Pequod* Ishmael the experiencing self does not know what will be the fate of him or the crew; but Ishmael the narrating self does know and therefore has the privilege of including in the narrative foreshadowings ("From that hour I clove to Queequeg like a barnacle; yea, till poor Queequeg took his last long dive" [chap. 13]), proleptic images (like the snow-hill phantom), and hints of what is to come ("in the sequel of the narrative, it will then be seen what like abandonment befell myself" [chap. 93]), as well as information that will later prove useful to the reader ("this peculiarity of the whale's eyes is . . . to be remembered by the reader in some subsequent scenes" [chap. 74]). A final point is that the valuations and interpretations that the experiencing self places on an event may tend to be different from the more distanced, mature, and possibly more insightful valuations and interpretations of the narrating self. The reader of *Moby-Dick* must learn to distinguish between the judgments and generalizations of the two Ishmaels and become aware of potential tensions between these views.[61]

What is Ishmael the character, the experiencing self, like? The novel's first chapter, with its striking conflations of the experiencing and narrating selves, is too complex to be helpful in answering this question, but the next twenty-one chapters are. The narrating self is seldom present in these chapters, which give the reader a strong impression of Ishmael the character through his own words and actions. These chapters describe the arrival of the younger Ishmael in New Bedford and his droll encounter with a savage in the Spouter-Inn. He also visits the Whaleman's Chapel, ponders the marble cenotaphs of whalemen lost at sea, and hears an impressive sermon by the celebrated Father Mapple. A warm bosom friendship quickly develops between him and the savage, Queequeg, and as a result Ishmael comes to feel "a melting in me" as he sits before the fire with his newfound pagan friend. And when the two are subsequently shown together in bed, smoking and talking, they seem "a cosy loving pair" on their "hearts' honeymoon" (chap. 10). They soon travel to Nantucket, where several more scenes are devoted to the two friends and where they both contract to serve on a whaling ship, the *Pequod,* which sets sail in chapter 22.

These early chapters reveal that the point of view of the younger Ishmael is in the main positive and upbeat. It is true that in addition to the suicidal rumblings in "Loomings," we hear talk about a "splintered heart and maddened hand," which are no longer "turned against the wolfish world" as a result of friendship with "the soothing savage" (chap. 10). But such telling has no counterpart in what the reader is shown about the character. We note, for example, his buoyantly optimistic hopes concerning death and immortality in the Whaleman's Chapel. And as the *Pequod* clears its harbor on a frigid winter night and meets the freezing spray of the north Atlantic, it nonetheless seems to the outsetting Ishmael that "many a pleasant haven" is in store for him, and "meads and glades so eternally vernal" that their grass remains "untrodden, unwilted" at midsummer (chap. 22). Ishmael the character, the younger, experiencing self, does reappear occasionally during the long middle section of *Moby-Dick.* In chapter 28, he mentions his "vague disquietude touching the unknown captain" and after the quarterdeck scene admits that he has succumbed to Ahab's dark spell: "I, Ishmael, was one of that crew; my shouts had gone up with the rest . . . and stronger I shouted . . . because of the dread in my soul . . .

Ahab's quenchless feud seemed mine" (chap. 41). In most of his subsequent appearances, however, Ishmael seems just as upbeat as he was in the opening chapter. In "The Mat-Maker" (chap. 47) and "The Monkey-Rope" (chap. 72), for example, we notice the same speculative perkiness he displayed in the Whaleman's Chapel and on the night the *Pequod* sailed. And in "A Squeeze of the Hand" (chap. 94) we find celebrated a cozy sense of manly love that recalls Ishmael's bonding with Queequeg in the Spouter-Inn. But these reappearances of the younger Ishmael are few and far between. After the *Pequod* sails in chapter 22 Ishmael the character recedes and his older narratorial counterpart becomes the dominant presence.

How does the older Ishmael, the narrator of *Moby-Dick,* compare with his younger self? The most obvious and important difference is that Ishmael the narrator has a more restless and wide-ranging speculative intelligence and a much darker vision of human life. A key juncture in *Moby-Dick* is chapter 23, "The Lee Shore," the point at which the voice and reflections of the older Ishmael begin to dominate the narrative. The chapter provides a short memorial for Bulkington, who, when briefly encountered at the Spouter-Inn, had just returned from a four-year voyage, but who sails with the *Pequod* soon after and is at its helm when it leaves Nantucket. Ishmael the narrator develops an elaborate image, turning on the contrast of land and sea, in order both to explain why Bulkington has irresistibly returned to sea and to suggest the exemplary heroism of his choice. It fared with him, says Ishmael, as with a storm-tossed ship that in order to avoid being wrecked on the shore, toward which it is being driven by a leeward wind, must try to keep away from "comfort, hearth-stone, supper, warm blankets, friends, all that's kind to our mortalities," and seek instead the safety of "the lashed sea's landlessness." All the items in the catalog of "what's kind to our mortalities" had been present in the earlier scenes on shore between Queequeg and Ishmael the character. But the "mortally intolerable truth" that the older Ishmael is concerned to drive home is that the shore is "treacherous, slavish"; that "all deep, earnest thinking" may be regarded as the intrepid attempt of the soul "to keep the open independence of the sea"; that the highest truth resides only in landlessness; and that "better it is to perish in the howling infinite, than to be ingloriously dashed upon the lee, even if that were safety!"

The symbolic contrast of land and sea dominates the reflections of the older Ishmael. One may say that while the younger Ishmael belongs essentially to the world of the shore, the vision of the older Ishmael reflects his experience of the sea and its physical and speculative perils. One of his most extended and rhetorically impressive elaborations of the land-sea image occurs in chapter 58, "Brit." It opens with a description of the *Pequod*'s sailing into "vast meadows of brit, the minute, yellow substance, upon which the Right Whale largely feeds. . . . We seemed to be sailing through boundless fields of ripe and golden wheat." The sight recalls and might seem to fulfill the hope of the younger Ishmael that pleasant meadows and glades would be encountered on his whaling voyage. But what follows in the chapter is the dark wisdom of the older Ishmael, not the wistful hopes of the younger. Both Ishmaels are interested in discovering the spiritual facts of which they believe natural facts to be the symbols. In "The Monkey-Rope," for example, the younger Ishmael, joined by a rope to Queequeg while the latter performs a hazardous task on a whale's slippery back, reflects that "we two, for the time, were wedded" (as they had been on shore at the Spouter-Inn) and that their condition of mutual dependence was "the precise situation of every mortal that breathes" (chap. 72). That is to say, even at sea the younger Ishmael found reminders of the values of the land. But in "Brit" the older Ishmael reflects that any resemblances between the land and the sea are tenuous or superficial. The sea is an "everlasting terra incognita," the "full awfulness" of which includes its "universal cannibalism." What then is the spiritual or human fact symbolized by the natural fact of the contrast between the sea and the "green, gentle and most docile earth"? Consider them both, the older Ishmael asks the reader, and "do you not find a strange analogy to something in yourself? For as this appalling ocean surrounds the verdant land, so in the soul of man there lies one insular Tahiti, full of peace and joy, but encompassed by all the terrors of the half known life. God keep thee! Push not off from that isle, thou canst never return!"

The advice at the end of this powerful passage is ironic in that the older Ishmael believes that the passage from the insular Tahiti within to the horrors of the half-known life without is inevitable and irreversible, and that failure to recognize this stamps one as "a provincial and sentimentalist in Truth" (chap. 76). Nor does the mature Ishmael believe that there is a beneficent God who can exempt one from this appalling rite of passage into adult consciousness. At this point, however, it is premature to generalize about the rhetoric and the vision of the mature Ishmael. We should first consider in some detail the salient features of his narration: his enormous resources of language, style, and voice; his concern with meaning and with the larger significance of natural facts; his awareness of, and direct addresses to, "you," the reader; and the various literary forms through which he presents his material.

V: *Ishmael as Narrator*

> But nature is a stranger yet;
> . . .
> To pity those that know her not
> Is helped by the regret
> That those who know her, know her less
> The nearer her they get.
>
> *Emily Dickinson*

One of the most distinctive features of Ishmael's narration in *Moby-Dick* is the variety of voices and styles he employs. We have already seen examples of his brooding meditative seriousness ("Loomings") and impassioned rhetoric ("The Lee Shore" and "Brit") and we shall later be examining a number of other examples of both. At other times, however, Ishmael can be much lighter, as in his tall-tale "extravaganzas" concerning Nantucket (chap. 14), his zany claim to be copying the dimensions of a whale's skeleton "verbatim from my right arm, where I had them tatooed" (chap. 102), his suggestion that cannibalism be considered a "spinal branch of phrenology" (chap. 80), or his buffoonish account of seeing "a curious involved worming and undulation in the atmosphere over my head" while composing "a little treatise on Eternity" in a thin-shingled attic room of an August noon after having drunk six cups of hot tea (chap. 85). In two places he parodies passages in Scoresby's *Account of the Arctic Regions;* in another passage he turns pseudoscholar in a high-spirited attempt to classify whales into folios, quartos, octavos, and so on. At other times his voice becomes that of the man-of-the-world raconteur, as in his narration of "The Town-Ho's Story," or where he tends to sound postprandially witty and cumbersomely genteel. Such passages contrast sharply with his intermittent phallic jokes and puns: the double entendres in the references to erections at the close of chapters 32 and 68; the reference to the Earl of Leicester presenting "another horn" than that of the narwhale to Queen Elizabeth (chap. 32); the gross pun on archbishopric at the end of chapter 95; and the reference to Queequeg pocketing his wooden, phallus-shaped idol Yojo "as carelessly as if he were a sportsman bagging a dead woodcock" (chap. 3).

The range of voice is matched by the wide spectrum of vocabulary. Ishmael is fascinated by words old, new, and invented: the very first word in the text of *Moby-Dick* is *etymology;* a philological footnote is supplied for *gallied* (chap. 87); a similar note in chapter 77 defines *quoin;* and in chapter 53 Ishmael delights to note that *gam* appears in neither Dr. Johnson's nor Noah Webster's dictionary and hastens to furnish a sample lexicon entry. In chapter 18 he describes the language of old Captain Bildad as consisting of "something of the salt sea . . . heterogeneously mixed with Scriptural and domestic phrases." Much of Ishmael's language in *Moby-Dick* may be similarly described as a heterogeneous mixture of sea terms (most of which, he observes, are "very happy and significant" [chap. 68]), abstract terms (mainly Latinate, and including a number of neologisms), and a variety of pungently demotic words, many of them distinctly American. Examples at the patrician end of the spectrum include *uninterpenetratingly, uncatastrophied, imminglings, leewardings, crescentric, curvicues, footmanism, halthinting, omnitooled, sultanism, pyramidical silence, child-magian thoughts, unensanguined, to serpentine,* and *to spiralize.* The plebian end includes *squitchy, higgledy-piggledy, skrimshander, Hay-Seed, squilgee, plumpuddinger, rigadig, slobgollion, quoggy, spiles, hypos, hunks, kelpy, lubber-like, chowder head, kedger, stiver,* and *fobbing.*

The range of diction in *Moby-Dick* is more than matched by the equally heterogeneous mixture of allusions, similes, and analogies with which the text is peppered. Their miscellaneous richness gives the novel much of its crackle and shows the constant play of Ishmael's agile and inquiring mind. These embellishments are also one of the principal ways in which the world of *Moby-Dick* is constantly being enlarged and expanded until it seems to include within its protean compass all parts of the globe and much of human history and thought. A sampling of Ishmael's extravagance and fecundity of allusion includes the following: mummified ibis birds found in ancient Egyptian tombs; Pythagoras's advice to his followers not to eat beans because they cause flatulence; the travels of John Ledyard by dogsled through Siberia and Mungo Park's journeys in the heart of Africa; the fact that bottled ale spoils in the Indies; the opposition of the ancient Ophites to the God of the Old Testament and their glorification of the serpent as the liberator of humanity; the Iroquois's midwinter sacrifice of the sacred White Dog; the theory of Lockean philosophers concerning primary and secondary qualities; Procopius's *History of His Own Time;* a horizontal burst boiler out of a Mississippi steamer; the title page of the original edition of Francis Bacon's 1605 *Advancement of Learning;* the skeleton of Jeremy Bentham; the deceptive appearance of recumbent elephants in the plains of India; the old American Indian characters chiseled on the palisades of the Upper Mississippi; Italian organ-boys holding a dancing ape by a long cord; the eager Israelites drinking at the bursting fountains that poured from the smitten rock; Michigan oxen dragging stumps of old oaks out of the wild woodlands; the nursery tale of the old woman who lived in a shoe; the great Heidelberg tun that held nearly fifty-thousand gallons of wine; the sudden movement of a small ice field when a herd of polar bears are scared from it into the sea; the exploits of Davy Crockett, Kit Carson, and Daniel Boone; the soldiers of Napoleon who during the Russian campaign turned their dead horses into tents and crawled into them; Eckermann's reaction to seeing the naked corpse of Goethe; Benedict Arnold at the battle of Saratoga; the sweetness of April grass butter; grated nutmeg swiftly stirred in a bowl of punch; and the potent digestion of an ostrich.

There is another kind of language used by Ishmael that figures importantly in *Moby-Dick.* In chapter 16 he describes the Quaker idiom of Nantucket whaling captains as "a bold and nervous lofty language." This language is principally evident in the speech of Captain Ahab; but Ishmael himself sometimes uses the same stylistic register, especially when his subject is Captain Ahab, complex psychological states, or Ahab-like speculations and broodings. For the presentation of these subjects simple similes or allusions will not suffice. Ishmael uses instead complex and startling images and boldly sustained paradoxes and oxymorons, one of which he tell-

ingly describes as "a furious trope" (chap. 41). We have already
encountered one of these complex images in "The Lee Shore." Another example is found in the description of "the broad madness
at work within Ahab's great natural intellect": his "special lunacy
stormed in his general sanity, and carried it, and turned all its con-
centrated cannon upon its own mad mark" (chap. 41). And this is
followed by an equally bold figure through which Ishmael attempts
to hint at a "larger, darker, deeper part" of Ahab's being: the as-
tonishing comparison of his psyche to the Hotel de Cluny in Paris,
which was built on the ruins of "the vast Roman halls of Thermes."

Sometimes Ishmael's complex images seem strained, more com-
plicated than complex, and even a little factitious. One example is
the attempt at the end of chapter 50 to give symbolic weight to the
shadowy figure of Fedallah through associating him with "the
ghostly aboriginalness of earth's primal generations," of the time
when devils as well as angels "indulged in mundane amours." Despite Ishmael's paragraph-long attempt to convey a sense of the
Parsee's "muffled mystery," his effort really boils down to little
more than what Stubb says in one short sentence: "I take that Fedallah to be the devil in disguise" (chap. 73). Other furious tropes,
however, like the ones describing Pip's madness in chapter 93, are
both more justified by their subject and more successful. Just before introducing the Hotel de Cluny image, Ishmael observes that
it is "vain to popularize profundities, and all truth is profound"
(chap. 41). But he is nonetheless determined to stretch his extraordinary stylistic resources to the fullest in order to convey as accurate a sense as he can of the psychological depth of his characters.

A final stylistic feature of Ishmael's narration is the magnificent
descriptions of midocean scenes that are among the most memorable features of *Moby-Dick*. Just as Ishmael is concerned to convey
through his furious tropes a sharply focused image of complex
states of mind, so through his verbal pictures is he concerned to
represent whales and whaling scenes as accurately and vividly as
he can—"to put the living sperm whale before you" (chap. 32) in
all its awesome power and magnificence. In chapter 55 ("Of the
Monstrous Pictures of Whales"), Ishmael reveals a self-conscious
awareness of the fact that he is giving his reader more accurate

pictures of whales "than those curious imaginary portraits of him which even down to the present day confidently challenge the faith of the landsman." The living whale, "in his full majesty and significance, is only to be seen at sea in unfathomable water," and it is only by "going a whaling yourself" that you can derive "even a tolerable idea of his living contour." Similarly, as Ishmael adds in the next chapter, only someone (like himself) who has been a whale hunter can furnish accurate "pictures of whaling scenes."

But in the pictures he paints, Ishmael is concerned with more than just fidelity to fact. He also wants to create striking images of the natural world that will have an aesthetic effect on the land-based reader—that will stimulate feelings of awe and sublimity and enlarge the reader's imaginative space in ways that will make him or her more receptive to the sense of "visable truth" that elsewhere in *Moby-Dick* Ishmael expresses through other artistic means. The scenes painted range in size from cameos to large, action-packed panoramas. Even the smallest canvas has great evocative power. Take, for example, the Turneresque description in chapter 54 of "the appalling beauty of the vast milky mass [of Moby Dick], that, lit up by a horizontal spangling sun, shifted and glistened like a living opal in the blue morning sea," or the sight in chapter 86 from a masthead "during a sunrise that crimsoned sky and sea [:] a large herd of whales in the east, all heading towards the sun, and for a moment vibrating in concert with peaked flukes." Ishmael compares this second picture to something in his literary rather than his personal experience: King Juba's account in Plutarch's *Morals* of "the military elephants of antiquity [who] often hailed the morning with their trunks uplifted in the profoundest silence." The parallel is striking, but in terms of their effect on the reader it is the fresh, first-hand description of the whales that vibrates resonantly in a way that the learned gloss does not.

Other pictures in *Moby-Dick* resemble tableaux: the whaler long absent from home, for example, with its bleached spectral appearance, the long channels of reddened dust along its sides, and its spars and rigging "like the thick branches of trees furred over with hoar-frost" (chap. 52); or "the enchanted crew" of the *Pequod* gazing at the pallid fire of the corposants, while, "relieved against the ghostly light, the gigantic jet negro, Daggoo, loomed up to thrice his real stature" (chap. 119). The conversation piece in chapter 96—the watch lounging on the windlass opposite the flames and dense smoke of the tryworks—is equally arresting and equally expressionistic. But it is the action canvasses that are the most memorable of the pictures in *Moby-Dick:* the red tide of blood pouring from all sides of a mortally wounded whale while the light of the slanting sun reflected from the crimson pond of blood on the sea reddens the faces of the whalemen closing in on their prey (chap. 62); the "incessant murdering of the sharks" in chapter 66; the sublime breaching of Moby Dick during the second day of the chase (chap. 134); the "nursing mothers of the whales" seen beneath the surface of the sea in chapter 87, their young resembling "human infants [who] while suckling will calmly and fixedly gaze away from the breast, as if leading two different lives at the same time"; and the superlative description of the *Pequod's* boats chasing a whale during "The First Lowering" (chap. 48), which gains much of its vividness from Ishmael's skillful deployment of land-associated images of the known and the familiar (a bowling green, glens and hollows, riding a horse, sledding, a hen and its brood, churning butter) to describe the unfamiliar and awesome perils of the whale hunt in midocean:

> It was a sight full of quick wonder and awe! The vast swells of the omnipotent sea; the surging, hollow roar they made, as they rolled along the eight gunwales, like gigantic bowls in a boundless bowling-green; the brief suspended agony of the boat, as it would tip for an instant on the knife-edge of the sharper waves, that almost seemed threatening to cut it in two; the sudden profound dip into the watery glens and hollows; the keen spurrings and goadings to gain the top of the opposite hill; the headlong, sled-like slide down its other side;—all these, with the cries of the headsmen and harpooneers, and the shuddering gasps of the oarsmen, with the wondrous sight of the ivory Pequod bearing down upon her boats with out-stretched sails, like a wild hen after her screaming brood;—all this was thrilling. Not the raw recruit, marching from the bosom of his wife into the fever heat of his first battle; not the dead man's ghost encountering the

first unknown phantom in the other world;—neither of these can feel stranger and stronger emotions than that man does, who for the first time finds himself pulling into the charmed, churned circle of the hunted sperm whale.

The first picture of a whaling scene that Ishmael offers the reader of *Moby-Dick* is not drawn from life. It is rather an ecphrasis (in this case a description of a work of visual art), the purpose of which is not realistic description but the exemplification of two of the principal thematic concerns of his narrative. The subject of the picture is a very large oil painting, "thoroughly besmoked, and in every way defaced," that hangs in the entry of the Spouter-Inn. Upon first seeing this "boggy, soggy, squitchy picture," with "a long, limber, portentous black mass of something" hovering in its center, Ishmael is struck by a certain "indefinite, half-attained sublimity about it" that makes him itch "to find out what that marvellous painting meant." First, however, he tries to answer a more basic question: what does the painting depict? He tries out several "bright, but, alas, deceptive" ideas and eventually realizes that the key to comprehension is identification of that black something in the picture's center. His "final theory, partly based upon the aggregated opinions of many aged persons with whom I conversed upon the subject," is that the painting depicts an exasperated whale (the black mass) in the act of impaling itself on the masts of a half-foundered ship during a great hurricane.

One thematic significance of Ishmael's scrutiny of the painting in the Spouter-Inn is that it exemplifies the difficulty, if not the impossibility, of arriving at certain knowledge even of empirical matters of fact. This is a subject to which Ishmael implicitly or explicitly returns over and over again in *Moby-Dick*. When the subject is whales, the incompleteness and uncertainty of human knowledge is repeatedly underlined. When examining the head of a right whale, for example, the nearer you come the more "it begins to assume different aspects, according to your point of view" (chap. 75). The only guarantee that Ishmael can give about his cetological endeavors is that they will necessarily be incomplete, for "any human thing supposed to be complete, must for that very reason infallibly be faulty" (chap. 32). The serious point behind the droll attempt to use a bibliographical system for classifying whales is that any classification will be imperfect and incomplete. There are similar implications in the "Etymology" and "Extracts" sections at the beginning of Moby-Dick; that, indeed, is their principal point. As the sub-sublibrarian of "Extracts" warns, his list, however extensive, provides only "a glancing bird's eye view" of its subject, not a "veritable gospel cetology." Even such a specific and delimited question as whether the spout of a sperm whale emits water or vapor can be answered with "no absolute certainty." If one persists in asking Ishmael to deliver an opinion on the subject, he can only reply: "My dear sir, in this world it is not so easy to settle these plain things. I have ever found your plain things the knottiest of all. And as for this whale spout, you might almost stand in it, and yet be undecided as to what it is precisely" (chap. 85). The best one can hope for, Ishmael remarks in another connection, is an approximate knowledge based on reasonable inferences and surmises: "Though the certainty of this criterion is far from demonstrable," he says, "yet it has the savor of analogical probability" (chap. 75).

The second thematic aspect that Ishmael's scrutiny of the painting at the Spouter-Inn exemplifies is his constant concern to find the meaning or significance that, he is convinced, resides in material things. This habitual activity of his mind is instanced several times early in Moby-Dick. In chapter 1 he says of the data he has brought together that "surely all this is not without meaning"; the same belief is reiterated six chapters later with reference to a different set of information: "All these things are not without their meanings"; and in the chapter after that the younger Ishmael exclaims of Father Mapple's prow-shaped pulpit: "What could be more full of meaning?" In a less sophomoric way, the older Ishmael, the narrator of Moby-Dick, is equally committed to the principle that natural facts are the symbols of spiritual facts: "And some certain significance lurks in all things," he asserts in chapter 99, "else all things are little worth."

Of course, Ishmael is not alone in his belief that natural facts are meaningful. In their different ways almost all the characters in

Moby-Dick share the same faith. At the crudest level, there is the crew of the *Pequod,* whose fascination with omens and portents exemplifies "that ignorance and superstitiousness hereditary to all sailors" (chap. 41), especially in times of heightened expectation and emotional stress. As Ishmael remarks of the crew just before Moby Dick is finally sighted: "Now almost the least heedful eye seemed to see some sort of cunning meaning in almost every sight" (chap. 130). Starbuck, the first mate of the *Pequod,* is also inclined to superstition, but in his case it "seems rather to spring, somehow, from intelligence than from ignorance. Outward portents and inward presentiments were his" (chap. 26). It is the combination of deep natural reverence and equally deep Christian faith that gives Starbuck his powers of spiritual (or symbolic) perception. Father Mapple, the other leading Christian in *Moby-Dick,* finds a "two-stranded lesson" (that is, two levels of symbolic meaning) in the biblical story of Jonah (chap. 9). In Gabriel, the mad sailor from the *Jeroboam,* the power of spiritual perception reaches an insane pitch: he regards the white whale as nothing less than "the Shaker God incarnated" (chap. 71). But, Ishmael aside, it is Captain Ahab who is the most conspicuous exponent in *Moby-Dick* of the principle that there is a meaning in all natural facts. At one point Ahab insists that all visible objects are but "pasteboard masks"—trivial phenomenal emblems of the large intangible forces behind them (chap. 36). Elsewhere he seems equally assured that from another point of view all external objects are symbols of mental or psychological states: "O Nature, and O soul of man!" he exclaims, "how far beyond all utterance are your linked analogies! not the smallest atom stirs or lives on matter, but has its cunning duplicate in mind" (chap. 70).

While all these characters share with Ishmael the belief in the meaningfulness of natural objects, his vision is different in one important particular: his awareness of the epistemological problem of the subjectivity of symbolic perception and of the consequent relativity of symbolic meaning. In speaking of the possible meanings of the "sublime" sight of a sperm whale breaching, Ishmael observes that "in gazing at such scenes, it is all in all what mood you are in; if in the Dantean, the devils will occur to you; if in that of Isaiah, the archangels" (chap. 86). Ishmael also knows what any careful reader of *Moby-Dick* does: that "to any monomaniac man, the veriest trifles capriciously carry meanings" (chap. 52). As for omens and portents, which he calls "admonitions and warnings," Ishmael knows that they are in reality predictions rather than warnings and "not so much predictions from without, as verifications of the foregoing things within" (chap. 36). That is to say, at least at the level of superstition, meaning does not inhere in the material object but is projected onto it by the observer.

Ishmael the narrator considers recognition of the subjective elements in the discovery of significance important enough to include in *Moby-Dick* a chapter that may be regarded as a primer in symbolic perception. "The Doubloon" (chap. 99) commences with another ecphrasis, the description of what is depicted on the visible side of the Equadorian doubloon that Ahab has nailed to the mast: the three mountain summits—one topped with a flame, another with a tower, the third with a crowing cock—with a segment of the zodiac arching over the three. In the first panel of the primer Ahab studies the doubloon and announces that every item on it represents himself. Like "a magician's glass," the doubloon "but mirrors back his own mysterious self." Starbuck's turn is next: for him the tripartite scene represents the Christian Trinity. The reaction of the second mate, Stubb, is the same as that of many undergraduate readers of *Moby-Dick:* he seeks the aid of secondary sources in finding meaning. With his almanac in hand, Stubb has no trouble in interpreting the zodiacal signs: "here is the life of man in one round chapter; and now I'll read it off, straight out of the book." The third mate, Flask, has no powers of symbolic perception; he looks at the doubloon and sees only the nine-hundred cigars he calculates it will buy. Three more renderings of the one text are given before it is the turn of Pip, whose first comment is not on the doubloon but on its various interpreters: "I look, you look, he looks; we look, ye look, they look." It shows that Pip has learned from the chapter the same lesson in the relative and inevitably pluralistic nature of symbolic perception that Ishmael wants the reader to learn.

But if this is the nature of symbolic perception, how can someone who is not a monomaniac and not self-deceived ever find a constant and unequivocal meaning in the particulars of the natural world? Will not all revelations or significances appear dubious, if not specious, to someone who recognizes the subjective element in all vision? Isn't the ungraspable phantom of life a chimera? When Ishmael says that some certain significance lurks in things, is he not really saying that meaning or significance *must* lurk in things because that is the only place they can lurk and that if there is no meaning in the natural world there can be no meaning or value in human life? Or is it rather that Ishmael feels that although there can be no certainty in symbolic perception there may be some "savour of analogical probability" similar to that which he seems to believe can be obtained from empirical perception? And are not the ever-alluring spirit-spout of chapter 51 and even the great white mass of the giant squid in chapter 59 awesomely convincing symbols of the ungraspable phantom of life—apparitions rather than chimeras?

It is still too early in our reading of *Moby-Dick* to try an answer to these questions. For one thing, the attempt should be made only after we have examined the vision of Captain Ahab, the dominant character in *Moby-Dick,* and compared it to Ishmael's vision. At this point it is more useful to identify the two ends of the spectrum of the mature Ishmael's meditative experience. One pole, which we might call the *all* feeling, is described in "The Mast-Head" (chap. 35). It is true that Ishmael the narrator is at a critical distance from his account of the visionary experience of "sunken-eyed young Platonists" like his earlier self. But it is also true that he knows the experience from the inside and that, as chapter 1 makes clear, what he describes is simply a particularly intense and transporting example of the deep-rooted human tendency to ocean reveries—"for as everyone knows, meditation and water are wedded for ever." In "The Mast-Head" Ishmael describes the dreamy and languorous expansion of consciousness that can overcome a person gazing out onto "the infinite series of the sea, with nothing ruffled but the waves." A "sublime uneventfulness" invests the gazer and in "this opium-like listlessness of vacant, unconscious reverie" the question of whether or not significance lurks in all things, and indeed all

other questions, are solved and dissolved in a pantheistic rapture
in which subject and object, outer and inner, immanent and transcendent, natural and spiritual, become one. The gazer "loses his
identity; takes the mystic ocean at his feet for the visible image of
that deep, blue bottomless soul, pervading mankind and nature;
and every strange, half-seen, gliding, beautiful thing that eludes
him . . . seems to him the embodiment of those elusive thoughts
that only people the soul by continually flitting through it." It is
the same Romantic experience that Emerson had described at the
beginning of *Nature* ("I become a transparent eye-ball; I am nothing; I see all; the currents of the Universal Being circulate through
me; I am part or particle of God") and what in the *Prelude,* published the year before *Moby-Dick,* Wordsworth described as those
blessed moments when

> such a holy calm
> Would overspread my soul, that bodily eyes
> Were utterly forgotten, and what I saw
> Appeared like something in myself, a dream,
> A prospect of the mind.[62]

The obverse of such ecstatic moments of oneness with the visible
world is the appalling vision of cosmic emptiness and hostility (the
nothing feeling) that concludes Ishmael's chapter on "The Whiteness of the Whale," the most sustained and rhetorically powerful
of all his meditations. In trying to explain the "vague nameless
horror" that at certain times was awakened in him by the thought
of Moby Dick, Ishmael begins by noting that it was "the whiteness
of the whale that above all things appalled me." In trying to discover why, he proceeds in a way typical of him: by attempting to
uncover the spiritual fact symbolized by the natural fact of whiteness. While this color has numerous associations with what is
"sweet, and honorable, and sublime," there is "an elusive something" lurking "in the innermost idea of this hue, which strikes
more of panic to the soul than that redness which affrights in
blood." He then considers polar bears, white sharks, albatrosses,
the "white steed of the Prairies," albino men, the violent white

squall that occurs in southern seas, the White Mountains of New Hampshire, the white buildings of Lima, the milky whiteness of a midnight sea, the snow-covered Andes, and an unbounded prairie sheeted with driven snow.

At the climax of the chapter Ishmael can still not say precisely what it is about whiteness that affects him so strongly; but he does know that he is powerfully affected and that the significance of the color has something to do with the knowledge of the demonism of the world, and with the recognition that while "in many of its aspects the visible world seems formed in love, the invisible spheres were formed in fright." It may be that by its very indefiniteness whiteness "shadows forth [i.e. symbolizes] the heartless voids and immensities of the universe, and thus stabs us from behind with the thought of annihilation, when beholding the white depths of the Milky Way"; or it may be that white is not so much a color as the visible absence of color—"a dumb blankness . . . a colorless all-color of atheism from which we shrink." Or, considering the theory of some natural philosophers that secondary qualities such as color exist only in the mind of the observer, we may come to feel either that "every stately and lovely emblazoning" of nature—"the sweet tinges of sunset skies and woods; yea, and the gilded velvets of butterflies, and the butterfly cheeks of young girls"—are like the cosmetics of a harlot, "whose allurements cover nothing but the charnel-house within," or that since the light that provides nature's hues is actually colorless in itself, if it operated without medium or matter it would touch all objects with its own blank tinge. When we ponder all this, says Ishmael, "the palsied universe lies before us like a leper; and like wilful travellers in Lapland, who refuse to wear colored and coloring glasses upon their eyes, so the wretched infidel gazes himself blind at the monumental white shroud that wraps all the prospect around him. And of all these things the Albino whale was the symbol. Wonder ye then at the fiery hunt?"

"The Whiteness of the Whale" meditation is not only an example of Ishmael's symbolic thinking; it is also a good illustration of his constant awareness of an audience and of his calculated and energetic efforts to get his readers to consider the deeper and darker implications of things by training them in speculation and

stimulating their imaginative involvement in his quest for the ungraspable phantom of life. In the climax of the chapter, the impassioned interrogations of which are studded with striking images,
what is of primary importance is not so much the discursive meaning of the passage as how forcefully it strikes the reader. "Wonder
ye then at the fiery hunt?"—the chapter's last and most crucial
question—has an imperative as well as interrogative urgency. What
is true of its concluding paragraph is true of the whole chapter: its
rhetorical (or persuasive) aspect is at least as important as what it
has to say, which is after all only one point (albeit a terminal one)
on Ishmael's spectrum.

In the second paragraph of "The Whiteness of the Whale" Ishmael is explicit about his concern to communicate with his audience. He must, if only "in some dim, random way, explain myself
. . . else all these chapters might be naught." They might be naught
if Ishmael is unsuccessful in getting the reader to see, feel, and
imagine along with him. He knows that the keys to sympathetic
identification lie in the reader's imagination and memory. "Without
imagination," he says, "no man can follow another into these
halls." Ishmael knows that "doubtless, some at least of the imaginative impressions about to be presented here have been shared by
most men." The problem is that "few perhaps were entirely con-
scious of them at the time, and therefore may not be able to recall
them now." One way of dealing with this situation would be pa-
tiently to try to stimulate the reader's memory and have him come
to recognize the congruity between his own faint past impressions
and Ishmael's vivid present ones. When he senses that the reader's
attention may be waning, however, Ishmael is quite prepared to
change his tactics: "But thou sayest, methinks this white-lead chapter about whiteness is but a white flag hung out from a craven soul;
thou surrenderest to a hypo, Ishmael." That is to say, Ishmael sup-
poses that his patient cataloging of images of whiteness is not
working as intended and that the reader is beginning to distance
himself from pusillanimous and unbalanced speculations. Ishmael's
response to his supposition is drastic and immediate. He abruptly
breaks the chain of images of affrighting whiteness, and introduces
the boldly emblematic image of the strong young colt, foaled in a

peaceful valley of Vermont, who succumbs to "phrensies of affright" when it smells the animal muskiness of a fresh buffalo robe
shaken behind it.

This image, like the other furious tropes deployed in *Moby-
Dick*, might be described as extravagant in the same positive sense
in which Thoreau employs the word to describe the mode of
expression he uses in *Walden* to break through "the narrow limits
of . . . daily experience, so as to be adequate to the truth of which
I have been convinced. . . . Why level downward to our dullest perception always, and praise that as common sense?"[63] Such verbal
extravagance needs a solid foundation, however, and in *Moby-
Dick* as in *Walden,* the bedrock of the narrative and its stylistic
embellishments—and the strategy used to secure the reader's sympathetic involvement—is a fully detailed documentary base. Over
and over again, Ishmael is at pains to insist on the factual accuracy
of his narrative: "I would fain advance naught but substantiated
facts" (chap. 25); "such things may seem incredible; but however
wondrous, they are true" (chap. 71); "I have seen Owen Chace,
who was chief mate of the Essex at the time of the tragedy; I have
read his plain and faithful narrative; I have conversed with his son"
(chap. 45). Since the sperm whale's life is "an unwritten life" (chap.
32), it is all the more necessary for Ishmael to include in his book
as much cetological information as he can so that "you [the reader]
will not fail to see, that . . . the most marvellous event in this book
[is] corroborated by plain facts of the present day" (chap. 45). As
Ishmael explains at the opening of "The Affidavit," the habits of
the sperm whale must be "still further and more familiarly enlarged
upon, in order to be accurately understood, and moreover to take
away any incredulity which a profound ignorance of the entire subject may induce in some minds, as to the natural verity of the main
points of this affair" (chap. 95).

While Ishmael is deeply concerned to persuade the reader of the
unvarnished truth of his narrative—"the plain facts" and "natural
verity"—he is equally concerned that the reader's interest not become fixated at the level of fact. This is well illustrated in "The
Town-Ho's Story" (chap. 54), a short story–length narrative inter-
polated by Ishmael into the larger text of *Moby-Dick*. Commen-

tators have provided a variety of explanations of the story of
Steelkilt and Radney's lethal antagonism and of its thematic relationship to the *Pequod*'s hunt for the white whale. But the most
suggestive reading is Heinz Kosok's, who regards "The Town-Ho's
Story" as a mirror for readers of *Moby-Dick*. The audience in Lima
to which Ishmael recounts the story is "a deliberate dramatization
of his own reading public." The circle of lounging gentlemen several times interrupt Ishmael's narrative because of their excessive
interest in superficial details irrelevant to the central concerns of
the story. Of course, Ishmael does not regard factual information
and circumstantial detail as unimportant: "I mention all these particulars," he tells his audience, "so that you may understand exactly how this affair stood between the two men." And he is most
concerned to have his listeners accept that the story "is in substance
and in its great items, true. I know it to be true. . . . I trod the ship;
I knew the crew." The problem is, Kosok points out, that the audience remains "far less concerned about the tale's spiritual meaning than its surface authenticity." [64]

"Natural verity" is not an end for Ishmael; it is a means. The
facts are used to provide a basis and an authenticating context for
the larger speculative issues in which he is passionately interested
and in which he wants his audience to become interested as well.
He wants the reader to move from the known and the familiar to
the unknown and unfamiliar, to leave the safety of the shore for
the liberating expanse of midocean, the domain of the great white
whale, the awesome natural fact that, even stripped of "supernatural surmisings," has enough in its "earthly make and incontest-
able character . . . to strike the imagination with unwonted power"
(chap. 41). For "unless you own the whale," as Ishmael insists at
the end of chapter 76, "you are but a provincial and sentimentalist
in Truth."

Ishmael usually addresses the reader in a quieter and less con-
frontational manner in order to stimulate imagination and memory
and help the reader to see that his own deeper feelings are different
from Ishmael's only in intensity. "If they but knew it," he observes
in the very first paragraph of chapter 1, "almost all men in their
degree, some time or other, cherish very nearly the same feelings

towards the ocean with me." In his "Ode on a Grecian Urn," Keats describes the ancient vase as having the power to "tease us out of thought / As doth eternity." In *Moby-Dick,* Ishmael, whose views on eternity are so unsettled and problematic, is rather concerned to tease the reader *into* thought. For this reason, among others, *Moby-Dick* is not, and does not aspire to be, a well-wrought urn, a self-complete work of art, or an object of aesthetic contemplation. Ishmael at one point observes that there is "an aesthetics in all things" (chap. 60), but the aesthetics of *Moby-Dick* are hardly that of Keats's ode. Ishmael's book is intentionally improvisational and open-ended, even ramshackle, as he more than once delights to point out. "Small erections," he exclaims at the end of chapter 32, "may be finished by their first architects; grand ones, true ones, ever leave the copestone to posterity. God keep me from ever completing anything. The whole book is but a draught—nay, but the draught of a draught." "I try all things," he says in chapter 79, "I achieve what I can."

Ishmael begins one chapter by disarmingly declaring that "there are some enterprises in which a careful disorderliness is the true method" (chap. 82). And near the beginning of another he explains that he does not care to perform the cetological part of his task "methodically." He will be content "to produce the desired impression by a separate citation of items" (chap. 45). In the main, Ishmael performs the other parts of his creative task in the same way. For this reason, the basic compositional unit and principal ordering device of *Moby-Dick* is the short, relatively self-contained chapter. Sometimes successive chapters form a sequence, as in the powerful concluding group of three chapters that describe the three-day chase for Moby Dick. There are also chapter clusters in which two to five (not necessarily successive) chapters are linked by themes or images. And there are balancing chapters either of opposites ("Loomings" and "Epilogue") or of similars ("The Quarter-Deck" and "The Candles").[65] Such loose groupings, however, do little to affect the reader's sense of *Moby-Dick* as a process rather than as a product, as a work in which one is as much interested in what the narrator will think of next as in what will happen next. And this is, of course, just as it should be in a book that has as a principal intention the stimulation of the reader's power of speculation and reflection.

The improvisational feel of Moby-Dick, however, should not keep one from realizing that there are complex calculations involved in Ishmael's mixture of documentary realism and speculative romance (the quest for the ungraspable phantom). Two of these calculations may be analogously suggested by the masterly way in which Ahab captains the Pequod. Ahab has a number of "yellowish sea charts" which he regularly consults in mapping his course. Although he is no more capable of absolute certainty than anyone else, with his charts and his vast experience he can "arrive at reasonable surmises, almost approaching to certainties" (chap. 44) concerning the likeliest time and place to encounter Moby Dick. Ahab's empirical powers give Ishmael's narrative of the Pequod's voyage a shape, direction, and climax (that is, a loose plot) that at the indeterminate speculative level (the level of meaning) it could not hope to possess.

Ahab also has to make careful psychological calculations in order to manipulate the crew of the Pequod. For him, the voyage has "one final and romantic object"—the encounter with Moby Dick. But Ahab knows that he cannot keep the attention of his crew constantly fixed on this ultimate goal during the course of a long voyage. To keep them pliant to his will, he must pay "a heedful, closely calculating attention to every minute atmospheric influence" to which the crew might be subjected and must "in a good degree continue true to the natural, nominal purpose" of the voyage (chap. 46). In the long middle section of Moby-Dick Ishmael does much the same thing for his reader. He prepares the reader for the final encounter with Moby Dick by providing details of whales and whaling through description of the normal activities of the crew. At the same time, he takes every opportunity provided by atmospheric conditions (the spirit-spout) or the symbolic potential of natural facts (the enchanted pond of nursing whales, squeezing the sperm, the fire of the tryworks) to keep warm the reader's interest in larger speculative issues. Then, from chapter 106 on, the pace of the book quickens as the cetological chapters are replaced by dramatic confrontations, soliloquies, symbolically charged scenes, and special effects like Fedallah's prophecies. Like the crew's, the reader's expectation becomes heightened "in the feverish eagerness of what seemed the approaching crisis of the voyage" (chap. 126).

The mixture of documentary and romance in *Moby-Dick* serves another important purpose as well. It keeps the reader from making serious mistakes about the nature of the work. As Ishmael remarks in chapter 45: "So ignorant are most landsmen of some of the plainest and most palpable wonders of the world, that without some hints touching the plain facts, historical and otherwise, of the fishery, they might scout at Moby Dick as a monstrous fable, or still worse and more detestable, a hideous and intolerable allegory." There is a close relationship between the kind of book *Moby-Dick* is and its epistemological premises, and, as Carlyle remarked, allegory "is the product of . . . certainty, not the producer of it." [66] For this reason alone, *Moby-Dick* could not be an allegory or a fable. It is rather a faithful account of a whaling voyage, which is at the same time, owing to the pressing intellectual and spiritual concerns of the far from certain retrospective narrator, a speculative romance in which (as has been said of Emily Dickinson's poetry) only the questions are definitive; the answers are always tentative.

If *Moby-Dick* is not a fable or an allegory, what is its generic classification? The answer is that the work is as generically miscellaneous as it is in other ways digressive and inclusive. As Nina Baym has observed, *Moby-Dick* seems "to include samples of every kind of generic writing."[67] They include the sermon; the short story; the occasional, scientific, and moral essay; satire; dictionary; encyclopedia; drama; dramatic monologue; manual; travelogue; tall tale; prophecy; and dream. In addition to fictional narrative with a documentary base and what I have been calling speculative romance, the two most important generic ingredients of *Moby-Dick* are epic and tragedy. They demand careful examination; but before turning our attention to them one other genre utilized in the book needs inspection because, unless certain distinctions are made, it can blur rather than help to focus the meanings of the work. That genre is the symbolic vignette or tableau. Two examples, already mentioned, occur at the beginning of "The Mat-Ma-ker" and "The Monkey-Rope" chapters. In both cases a realistically presented situation takes on a symbolic dimension, as the younger Ishmael allows his mind to play over it. In the former example, the mat being woven by Queequeg and Ishmael becomes the Loom of Time—its warp is necessity, its shuttle is free will, and the wooden sword with which it is intermittently struck is chance. The transference here from literal to symbolic is an aspect of the familiar Romantic tendency to interpret natural facts as symbols of spiritual facts, the agent of conceptual transference being the human observer. The same process is at work in "The Doubloon" chapter, only there Ishmael's response to natural fact is replaced by the response of several members of the *Pequod*'s crew to an arti-fact; and the purpose of the exercise is to underline the key epis-temological point that meaning is dependent on the predisposition of the perceiver.

Some of the symbolic vignettes in *Moby-Dick*, however, cannot be described in the same way and seem to operate on different principles. Two examples are Tashtego's plunge into the whale's head and his subsequent obstetrical delivery by Queequeg, and Tashtego's nailing a sky hawk as well as the flag of Ahab to the mast of the *Pequod* just before it sinks. Of course, both episodes are patently symbolic and no attentive reader of *Moby-Dick* will have difficulty in supplying suggestions concerning their nonliteral meanings. In neither case, however, do we have a plausible natural fact, activity, or artifact given symbolic meaning by a single per-ceiver within the novel. In both cases there is a distortion of the realistic surface in order to provide what might be called literary or authorial symbols. These vignettes are not univocal and they can be seen to relate to various important thematic strands in the book. But they do seem contrived, gratuitous, and unresonant in ways that recall D. H. Lawrence's comment about *Moby-Dick* contain-ing "exoteric symbolism of profound significance, and of consid-erable tiresomeness."[68]

VI: Epic and Tragedy

> The question may be raised whether the Epic or
> Tragic mode of imitation is the higher.
>
> *Aristotle, Poetics*

Epic and tragedy, traditionally held to be the highest literary genres, are the principal ingredients that Ishmael uses to give shape, resonance, and significance to his re-creation of his experiences on board the *Pequod*. They are also the two aspects of *Moby-Dick* that highlight the self-conscious, experimental boldness of Ishmael the narrator, whose vast ambition is to write a mighty book even though his material seems distinctly unpromising—as he implicitly admits in chapter 41: "Here, then, was this grey-headed, ungodly old man, chasing with curses a Job's whale round the world, at the head of a crew, too, chiefly made up of mongrel renegades, and castaways, and cannibals."

Let us consider the epic mode of imitation first. Ishmael makes no attempt to disguise his efforts to surround the occupation of whaling with "aesthetically noble associations" (chap. 24) and to show it to be more than just a "slatternly, untidy business" (chap. 92). He takes every opportunity to call attention to "the honor and glory of whaling" (chap. 82), to elevate the men of the *Pequod* to heroic stature, and to raise their nineteenth-century commercial activities to the level of quest. One way of doing so is to play up the awesomeness of the object of the *Pequod*'s hunt. The sperm whale in general is "without doubt, the largest inhabitant of the globe" (chap. 32). It can attain a weight of ninety tons, which is considerably more than "the combined population of a whole village of one thousand one hundred inhabitants" (chap. 103). The sperm whale is also a creature of great antiquity and primeval associations: it "swam the seas before the continents broke water" (chap. 105); it is "the mightiest animated mass that has survived the flood; most monstrous and most mountainous! That Himalehan, salt-sea Mastodon" (chap. 14). The whale is similarly of great mythological antiquity; through contemplation of it one is "borne back to that wondrous period, ere time itself can be said to have begun; for time began with man." In that "antemosaic" period (chap. 104), before later gods became enthroned "in the now egotistical sky" (chap. 79), "the whole world was the whale's"; it was "king of creation." And even in the present day it retains these "sublime," "god-like" associations. In gazing at its immensely amplified brow, "you feel the Deity and the dread powers more forcibly than in beholding any other object in living nature" (chap. 79).

No wonder, then, that Moby Dick in particular, the great albino sperm whale, has become the subject of "all manner of morbid hints, and half-formed foetal superstitions of supernatural agencies." One can perhaps discount the superstitious surmises that the whale is ubiquitous and immortal; but it is not so easy to deny the "specific accounts" that it has "over and over again evinced in his assaults" an "unexampled, intelligent malignity" (chap. 41). Nor are these surmises of godlike power and supernatural force in any way lessened by firsthand observation. Here, for example, is the awe-inspiring appearance of the great sea beast on the final day of the chase:

> Suddenly the waters around them slowly swelled in broad circles; then quickly upheaved, as if sideways sliding from a submerged berg of ice, swiftly rising to the surface. A low rumbling sound was heard; a subterraneous hum; and then all held their breaths; as bedraggled with trailing ropes, and harpoons, and lances, a vast form shot lengthwise, but obliquely from the sea. Shrouded in a thin drooping veil of mist, it hovered for a moment in the rainbowed air; and then fell swamping back into the deep. Crushed thirty feet upwards, the waters flashed for an instant like heaps of fountains, then brokenly sank in a shower of flakes. (chap. 135)

This is, as one commentator has said, "the primitive, unexplained world of Grendel's lake" in the Anglo-Saxon epic *Beowulf*, the place "where poetry begins."[69]

Just as the sperm whale is the king of midocean, so Ishmael claims that its American hunters are the elite of the whaling industry. "Our heroic Nantucketers" (chap. 24), the first "to harpoon with civilized steel the great Sperm Whale" (chap. 101), belong to an "emblazoned . . . fraternity" that includes among its old boys Perseus, St. George, Hercules, Jonah, and Vishnu (chap. 82). As the sperm whale is the most powerful of creatures, so during the southern whaling voyage ("by far the longest of all voyages now or ever made by man" [chap. 33]) does the whaleman face perils compared to which even the dangers of the soldier's profession seem mild: "for what are the comprehensible terrors of man compared with the interlinked terrors and wonders of God" (chap. 24).

Such claims may sound hyperbolic, if not factitious; they are certainly less striking than the places where Ishmael points up the primitive barbaric heroism of the hunters of the sperm whale, "that wild Scandinavian vocation on which I had so abandonedly embarked" (chap. 28). When Ishmael enters the Spouter-Inn in chapter 3, after examining the large oil painting he turns his attention to the opposite wall of the entry:

> [It] was hung all over with a heathenish array of monstrous clubs and spears. Some were thickly set with glittering teeth resembling ivory saws; others were tufted with knots of human hair; and one was sickle-shaped, with a vast handle sweeping round like the segment made in the new-mown grass by a long-armed mower. You shuddered as you gazed, and wondered what monstrous cannibal and savage could ever have gone death-harvesting with such a hacking, horrifying implement. Mixed with these were rusty old whaling lances and harpoons all broken and deformed. Some were storied weapons. With this once long lance, now wildly elbowed, fifty years ago did Nathan Swain kill fifteen whales between a sunrise and a sunset. And that harpoon—so like a corkscrew now—was flung in Javan seas, and run away with by a whale, years afterwards slain off the Cape of Blanco.

And in the public room beyond the entry stands "the vast arched bone of the whale's jaw, so wide, a coach might almost drive beneath it." The same mixture of the primitive and the legendary is played up in the initial description of the *Pequod* in chapter 16, her bulwark "garnished like one continuous jaw, with the long sharp teeth of the sperm whale" and her tiller "curiously carved from the long narrow lower jaw of her hereditary foe." The ship, says Ishmael, announces its history and its purpose in a way that recalls the "carved buckler or bedsted of Thorkill-Hake," the eleventh-century Icelandic hero whose great deeds were carved over his bed and on a stool before his highseat.

Of the sailors on the *Pequod*, it is the three pagan harpooneers who most vividly embody the primitive splendor of a heroic calling: the mysteriously tattooed and superstitious Queequeg, from the South Pacific; Tashtego, the American Indian, whose long sable hair, high cheekbones, and black eyes "sufficiently proclaimed him an inheritor of the unvitiated blood of those proud warrior hunters, who, in quest of the great New England moose, had scoured, bow in hand, the aboriginal forests of the main"; and Daggoo, the "gigantic, coal-black, negro-savage, with a lion-like tread," who retains all the "barbaric virtues" of his African past. Captain Ahab is also said to exemplify the virtues of a primitive heroic age. One hears of "bold dashes of character, not unworthy of a Scandinavian sea-king" (chap. 16); and even the stool made of whale bone on which he sits when smoking his pipe reminds Ishmael that "in old Norse times, the thrones of the sea-loving Danish kings" were made of the tusks of the narwhale (chap. 30). These narratorial attempts to associate Ahab with the heroes of the ancient sagas of northern Europe are, however, less effective in raising the action of *Moby-Dick* to the level of primitive epic than are the efforts of Ahab himself who, in making the crew of the *Pequod* the instrument of his will, knows how to use heroic motifs—the glitter of gold, the swearing of oaths, and the ritual drinking from a shared vessel—to raise his motley crew to the level of heroic action.

Other examples could be cited of Ishmael's difficulties and imperfect success in working heroic motifs into his material. One big problem is that the documentary realism of the narrative inevitably calls attention to unheroic and aheroic aspects of the crew, like the homosexual shenanigans in "Midnight, Forecastle" (chap. 40), or Flask's cruel treatment of the "horribly pitiable" old whale (chap.

82). Or consider the fact that Tashtego and Daggoo are present in *Moby-Dick* much less frequently than is Stubb, the fully competent but entirely unheroic second mate, who seems, so to speak, to have boarded the *Pequod* from the pages of Dickens rather than from those of saga or epic. The fact that Ishmael is as successful as he is working heroic motifs into his material is owing to the close connection in heroic poetry between the practical and the elevated, as well as to the special conditions of a ship on a long ocean voyage. In his *Epic and Romance*, W. P. Ker explained that

> the form of society in an heroic age is aristocratic and magnificent. At the same time, this aristocracy differs from that of later and more specialised forms of civilisation. . . . The great man is the man who is best at the things with which every one is familiar. . . . The great man is a good judge of cattle; he sails his own ship. . . . This relation between captain and men may be found, accidentally and exceptionally, in later and more sophisticated forms of society. . . . In later times it is only by a special favour of circumstances, as for example by the isolation of shipboard from all larger monarchies, that the heroic relation between the leader and the followers can be repeated. As society becomes more complex and conventional, this relation ceases. . . . An heroic age may be full of all kinds of nonsense and superstition, but its motives of action are mainly positive and sensible,—cattle, sheep, piracy, abduction, merchandise, recovery of stolen goods, revenge. The narrative poetry of an heroic age, whatever dignity it may obtain either by its dramatic force of imagination, or by the aid of its mythology, will keep its hold upon such common matters, simply because it cannot do without the essential practical interests, and has nothing to put in their place, if kings and chiefs are to be represented at all. The heroic age cannot dress up ideas or sentiments to play the part of characters. If its characters are not men they are nothing, not even thoughts or allegories; they cannot go on talking unless they have something to do; and so the whole business of life comes bodily into the epic poem.[70]

In addition to its connections with sagas and heroic poetry in general, *Moby-Dick* also has some of the conventional features of the classical epic: it is ample and indeed worldwide in scale, and is similarly inclusive in the knowledge and learning it deploys; its narrative style is frequently elevated and distanced from ordinary speech; and its action involves what to all intents and purposes may be regarded as superhuman deeds in battle. There are other traditional epic features in *Moby-Dick*, two of which I want to examine in brief and consider against the background of the various attempts made by major nineteenth-century writers to produce a modern epic. A list of works that are to a greater or lesser degree epic in ambition would include Blake's *Jerusalem*, Wordsworth's *Prelude*, Byron's *Don Juan*, Keats's *Hyperion* and *The Fall of Hyperion*, Carlyle's *French Revolution*, Whitman's *Song of Myself*, Tennyson's *Idylls of the King*, Browning's *The Ring and the Book*, Tolstoy's *War and Peace*, and George Eliot's *Middlemarch*.

One of these traditional features is the address to the epic muse, who is beseeched to inspire the writer in his great undertaking. Ishmael's version of this invocation occurs at the end of chapter 26. It is addressed not to a classical deity but to "thou just Spirit of Equality, which hast spread one royal mantle of humanity over all my kind!" This figure is the "great democratic God," who in Ishmael's litany of supplication is said to have inspired not only Bunyan and Cervantes but also Andrew Jackson, the American democrat who rose from backwoods cabin to the presidency. In the same passage Ishmael explains that the "august dignity" he treats in his book "is not the dignity of kings and robes." One can rather see it shining "in the arm that wields a pick or drives a spike; that democratic dignity which, in all hands, radiates without end from God . . . the centre and circumference of all democracy." It is this democratic muse that Ishmael hopes can solve the problems involved in raising his subject matter to a heroic level. "If then," he continues, "to meanest mariners, and renegades and castaways, I shall hereafter ascribe high qualities, though dark; weave round them tragic graces; if even the most mournful, perchance the most abased among them all, shall at times lift himself to the exalted mounts," the reason is that all the men of the *Pequod* belong to the "kingly commons."

This invocation reminds one of some of the less temperate encomia of Whitman and other literary nationalists of mid-nine-teenth-century America. And since Ishmael invokes this democratic muse nowhere else in *Moby-Dick,* one might even want to doubt his sincerity in this passage. There is no doubt, however, that the passage illustrates Ishmael's self-consciousness about writing an epic work in the nineteenth century. Another important place where Ishmael's self-consciousness becomes so intense that it breaks through the narrative surface is at the end of chapter 33: "But Ahab, my Captain, still moves before me in all his Nantucket grimness and shagginess; and in this episode touching Emperors and Kings, I must not conceal that I have only to do with a poor old whale-hunter like him; and therefore, all outward majestical trappings and housings are denied me. Oh, Ahab! what shall be grand in thee, it must needs be plucked at from the skies, and dived for in the deep, and featured in the unbodied air!" As in the "great democratic God" passage, Ishmael is here aware that his subject is not elevated by his social position: Ahab has "no outward majes-tical trappings and housings." Ishmael must therefore supply this lack through his own creative efforts—by investing Ahab with dig-nity and grandeur through images drawn from the natural world. Examples abound; they include Ahab's presiding at dinner like a "mute, maned sea lion on the white coral beach" and his living "as the last of the Grisly Bears lived in settled Missouri" (chap. 34). He shouts once like a "heart-striken moose" (chap. 36) and anoth-er time in an "old lion voice" (chap. 52); he is likened to "some lone, gigantic elm" (chap. 119) and to the unsetting polar star (chap. 130); and his madness is once compared to the Hudson Riv-er flowing through the Highland gorge (chap. 41). And when he is injured on the first day of the chase "nameless wails came from him, as desolate sounds from out ravines" (chap. 133).

Both these reflexive passages are examples of the general tenden-cy in the nineteenth century for the epic subject to become inter-nalized, the subject becoming either the writer's attempt to write an epic or the preparations for the attempt.[71] But there is a more particular explanation for Ishmael's literary difficulties in giving Ahab epic stature. It is the same as the reason for his epistemolog-ical difficulties: meaning and significance do not reside in the object or character itself, but are projected onto it by the perceiver. As a result, like "all things," Ahab's status is indeterminate and problematic. Depending on one's point of view Ahab can be either a poor old whale hunter, a "Catskill eagle" (chap. 96), an "anaconda of an old man" (chap. 40), or even, to recall two striking images used at the end of chapter 44, Christ or Prometheus.

One new feature of several nineteenth-century epic attempts was their factual, even documentary basis. John Stuart Mill opened his review of Carlyle's *French Revolution* by insisting that the work was "not so much a history, as an epic poem; and notwithstanding, or even in consequence of this, the truest of histories";[72] and Browning began his *Ring and the Book* by describing the discovery of his documentary source, the old yellow book, and insisting more than once that his epic matter was "pure crude fact." And we have already examined Ishmael's claims about the factual truth of his narrative. But one of the principal conventions of traditional epic had been supernatural agency or divine intervention. The question then arises: is it possible to have both a commitment to fact and instances of supernatural causation in the same work? Indeed, is it any longer possible to employ supernatural causation convincingly in any imaginative work in a century characterized by what has been called the disappearance of God? In *The French Revolution,* as in *War and Peace,* the force of history provides a kind of superhuman agency. And it has been observed of *The Ring and the Book* that the Pope's monologue in book 10 provides a perspective that comes close to being transcendent and absolute.

In *Moby-Dick,* as in Tennyson's *Idylls of the King,* the question of supernatural causation is handled in a different way. As Dwight Culler observed of Tennyson's poem: "One would not have thought it possible, but Tennyson has written an entire poem on King Arthur and his knights without one single instance of magic or the supernatural offered on the poet's own authority."[73] The same is true of *Moby-Dick:* for events, effects, or forces that seem supernatural there is always the possibility of a natural or psychological explanation. The "silvery jet" of the spirit-spout, the "flitting apparition" that "seemed for ever alluring us on" (chap. 51), may seem as otherworldly as the "pallid fire" of the corposants (chap. 119), which impresses even Stubb. But while these portentous sights allure, enchant, and awe the crew of the *Pequod*, both are explicable as natural phenomena. Like Moby Dick, they can be stripped of their "supernatural surmisings" and explained in strictly "earthly" terms (chap. 41). The same can be said of the notion of an external Fate. As we have seen, Ishmael entertains this notion in the opening chapter of *Moby-Dick* and in other places later. But its principal propagator is Ahab, who is never more rhetorically impassioned than when on the second day of the chase he tells Starbuck that everything that is happening or will happen to the *Pequod* has been predestined by a higher power: "This whole act's immutably decreed. 'Twas rehearsed by thee and me a billion years before this ocean rolled. Fool! I am the Fates' lieutenant; I act under orders" (chap. 134). By this late point in *Moby-Dick*, however, the reader knows the workings of Ahab's mind well enough to consider his belief in an external, superhuman causation evidence of his attempt to project onto the universe the internal, psychological necessity that is compelling him and his crew to their destruction. And the last paragraph of *Moby-Dick* may be said to present the reader just what was offered in "Loomings": not an unequivocal endorsement of Fate, but alternative possibilities that in the nature of things cannot be reconciled, any more than in the nineteenth century supernatural causation can be unequivocally asserted.

One unusual epic feature of *Moby-Dick* is its hero: Ahab is neither successful nor predominantly sympathetic. In this regard, the figure whom he most closely resembles is Satan in *Paradise Lost*, the great Puritan epic of seventeenth-century England. Milton's poem was unquestionably an important influence on *Moby-Dick*, as it was on most other epic attempts during the nineteenth century. The influence is particularly visible in Ishmael's depiction of Ahab. The captain's heroic defiance of an implacable foe that "tasks me [and] heaps me" (chap. 36) recalls Satan's determination not to submit to God; similarly Ahab's "fatal pride" (chap. 124) owes something to the "obdurate pride and steadfast hate" of Milton's fallen archangel. Ahab says that "all loveliness is anguish to me, since I can n'er enjoy" (chap. 37), while for Satan, "all good to me becomes / Bane." And when Ahab blasphemously baptizes the harpooneers' barbs "non . . . in nomine patris, sed in nomine diaboli" (chap. 113), the reader inevitably recalls Satan's "Evil be thou my Good." Other resemblances between Ahab and Satan could be remarked, particularly those found in their soliloquies.

The word *soliloquy*, however, belongs primarily to a literary kind very different from that of epic, and before examining Ahab's soliloquies closely it is first necessary to change the generic focus. The reason Ahab speaks soliloquies is not that Milton's Satan does. It is because both these great imaginative creations are closely modeled on the tragic heroes of Elizabethan drama, particularly Shakespeare's greatest tragedies. At the end of chapter 33, Ishmael refers to himself as a "tragic dramatist." Hundreds of pages later he begins the brief epilogue to *Moby-Dick* by saying "The drama's done." In between, Ishmael periodically employs dramatic conventions with what must initially seem a willful disregard for the reader's expectations. Some chapters are written up as if for the stage, for example "The Quarter-Deck," the first grand public scene in *Moby-Dick,* which begins with a stage direction ("Enter Ahab; Then all") and in which Ahab at times speaks in what is virtually blank verse.[74] Other chapters consist wholly or in part of soliloquies, in which different characters either lay bare their thoughts or reveal what they think about other characters. Still other chapters are presented as dramatic scenes, with bracketed stage directions in italics, as in the standard printed play format. The most extended example is chapter 41, "Midnight Forecastle," the very title of which is a stage direction, as are the titles of some other chapters.

Altogether there are thirteen chapters in *Moby-Dick* in which Ishmael advances the action and the argument of his book as a playwright supplying the reader with scripts. This baker's dozen might be thought evidence of Melville's belated recognition of the tragic potentialities of his story and of his slapdash, all-my-books-are-botches method of composition. But the better way to think about these scenes is to see them as part of the attempt by Ishmael, the self-conscious narrator, to find meaning and significance in his retrospective account of his experiences on the *Pequod.* In these chapters, Ishmael uses a dramatic lens to bring into focus certain important aspects of his material—both for his own clarification and as a way of more effectively communicating the meanings of his story to the reader. That this dramatic focus is discontinuous and tentative is only to be expected of a narrator whose book, as we have already seen in other connections, is as much a process as a product and whose informing theme is the search for meaning and significance. There is also an important expressive aspect to Ishmael's use of tragic conventions—especially the soliloquy. It enables him to articulate some of his own complex feelings, passions, and speculative urges by projecting them onto another character. From this point of view, Ahab, the resolute man of action, is a kind of Yeatsian mask through which Ishmael, the passive, reflective narrator, can give voice to some of his deepest feelings and darkest thoughts. This symbiosis is the reason that at times, as we shall see, it is so difficult to distinguish Ishmael's thoughts from Ahab's and even to tell who of the two is speaking.

In chapter 16, one sees Ishmael enacting (or reenacting) his shock of recognition at Ahab's potential as the hero of a tragic drama. (It is one of the most important of the self-conscious reflexive passages in *Moby-Dick*.) Ishmael has been generalizing about Captains Peleg and Bildad and the ways in which their Quaker peculiarities have been "anomalously modified" by the alien experience of hunting whales, when he is suddenly struck by a different thought, one that triggers his creative imagination. Thinking out loud, with growing excitement, he hurriedly sketches the main lines of what will eventually become the fully detailed and richly complex portrait of Ahab as tragic hero:

> So that there are instances among them of men, who, named with Scripture names—a singularly common fashion on the island—and in childhood naturally imbibing the stately dramatic thee and thou of the Quaker idiom; still, from the audacious, daring, and boundless adventure of their subsequent lives, strangely blend with these unoutgrown peculiarities, a thousand bold dashes of character, not unworthy of a Scandinavian sea-king, or a poetical Pagan Roman. And when these things unite in a man of greatly superior natural force, with a globular brain

and a ponderous heart; who has also by the stillness and seclu-
sion of many long night-watches in the remotest waters, and beneath constellations never seen here at the north, been led to
think untraditionally and independently; receiving all nature's
sweet or savage impressions fresh from her own virgin voluntary
and confiding breast, and thereby chiefly, but with some help
from accidental advantages, to learn a bold and nervous lofty
language—that man makes one in a whole nation's census—a
mighty pageant creature, formed for noble tragedies. Nor will it
at all detract from him, dramatically regarded, if either by birth
or other circumstances, he have what seems a half wilful over-
ruling morbidness at the bottom of his nature. For all men trag-
ically great are made so through a certain morbidness. Be sure of
this . . . all mortal greatness is but a disease.

Shakespeare's tragic heroes are the principal points of reference
and models used by Ishmael in transforming Ahab from a Quaker
whaling captain into "a mighty pageant creature." This is clear
from the large number of allusions to, and echoes and derivations
of, Shakespeare's tragedies, particularly *King Lear, Macbeth,* and
Hamlet. There are some obvious similarities, for example, between
Ahab and Lear, particularly the way in which both of them, "tor-
mented into desperation, [speak] the sane madness of vital truth"
(to recall Melville on Lear in the "Hawthorne and His Mosses"
essay). Ahab's "Oh, take medicine, take medicine" (chap. 120)
echoes Lear's "Take physic, Pomp"; when the former exclaims
"Who's to doom, when the judge himself is dragged to the bar"
(chap. 132), we remember the old king's fulminations about justice
in act 4; and when in the same chapter Ahab tells Starbuck that
"By heaven, man, we are turned round and round in this world,
like yonder windlass," we recall the great image Lear uses in telling
Cordelia that he is bound "Upon a wheel of fire, that mine own
tears / Do scald like molten lead" (act 4, scene 7). And, of course,
the relationship of Ahab and the mad Pip is modelled on that of
Lear and the Fool. The presence of *Macbeth* is perhaps even more
strongly felt in *Moby-Dick.* Ahab and Macbeth share dreams that
disrupt sleep, the torture of increasing isolation from humanity,
and the recognition, made in reflective, negative soliloquies, that

naught remains for them but to go on. In both works the natural order seems to protest their impious acts. And the three prophecies of Fedallah and their ironic fulfillment are all too closely modeled on the three prophecies of the witches in *Macbeth*.

If Ahab's soliloquies resemble Macbeth's in some ways, in others they resemble Hamlet's, particularly perhaps in their "short, quick probings at the very axis of reality," to cite "Hawthorne and His Mosses" again. In his notes on *Hamlet,* Coleridge had described the title character's mental disturbance as the result of "an over-balance in the contemplative faculty" that had caused his thoughts and the images of his fancy to become far more vivid to him than his actual perceptions, which when exposed to his contemplations instantly acquired "a form and a color not naturally their own." Coleridge went on to describe Shakespeare's technique in more general terms: "Now one of Shakespeare's modes of creating characters is, to conceive any one intellectual or moral faculty in morbid excess, and then to place himself, Shakespeare, thus mutilated or diseased, under given circumstances."[75] It is clear from the striking similarities in language between this description and the close of the passage from chapter 16 quoted above, that Ishmael has read not only *Hamlet* but also Coleridge on *Hamlet*. Indeed, he echoes Coleridge again in chapter 41 when he describes Ahab as "deliriously transferring" his idea of an "intangible malignity" to the white whale and then in his "frantic morbidness," pitting himself, "all mutilated, against it." It is this Coleridgean insight into the character and the characterization of Shakespeare's tragic heroes that is the most important of the Shakespearean appropriations used by Ishmael in making Ahab not only into a nineteenth-century American tragic hero but also into one of the premier characters in world literature.

VII: *Ahab*

Dark'n'd so, yet shone
Above them all th' Arch-Angel: but his face
Deep scars of Thunder had intrencht, and care
Sat on his faded cheek, but under Brows
Of dauntless courage, and considerate Pride
Waiting revenge.

Milton, Paradise Lost

While Ahab is the creation of Ishmael, he is not simply a projection of the narrator's intellectual and spiritual vexations any more than he is simply a bricolage of Shakespearean odds and ends, pieces of Milton's Satan, and bits of Byron's dark heroes. He is rather one of the comparatively few original characters in fiction, even if we accept the rigorous definition of *original* put forward by the narrator of *The Confidence-Man,* Melville's last novel. In the forty-fourth chapter of that work, the narrator argues that fictional characters who are thought to be original "can hardly be original in the sense that Hamlet is, or Don Quixote, or Milton's Satan"; they are rather "novel, or singular, or striking, or captivating, or all four at once"—but not original. In almost all characters so designated, there is "something prevailingly local, or of the age," as well as "something personal—confined to itself." The original character, on the other hand, is in essence "like a revolving Drummond light, raying away from itself all round it—everything is lit by it, everything starts up to it (mark how it is with Hamlet), so that, in certain minds, there follows upon the adequate conception of such a character, an effect, in its way, akin to that which in Genesis attends upon the beginning of things."[76] Unlike Hamlet, however, Ahab is presented through the medium of a self-conscious experimental narrator; and in examining the source and magnitude of his illumination we shall have at the same time to consider the different prisms through which the light is refracted. That is to say, the character and the characterization of Ahab will have to be treated in tandem.

The initial presentation of Ahab occurs in chapters 28 ("Ahab"), 29 ("Enter Ahab; to Him, Stubb"), and 30 ("The Pipe"). Before this, Ishmael picks up some information about the captain of the *Pequod* from Captain Peleg in chapter 16 and from Elijah, the ominous beggarlike stranger, in chapter 19. The effect of these tidbits on the reader is the same as their effect on Ishmael: they stimulate curiosity about Ahab and arouse a certain apprehension. After talking with Peleg, Ishmael says he felt "a sympathy and a sorrow for [Ahab], but for I don't know what, unless it was the cruel loss of his leg. And yet I also felt a strange awe of him: but that sort of awe . . . was not exactly awe; I do not know what it was. But I felt it" (chap. 16). And after listening to the "half-hinting, half-revealing" talk of Elijah, all kinds of "vague wonderments and half-apprehensions" stir in Ishmael's mind (chap. 19). This "vague disquietude touching the unknown captain" becomes much more intense when in chapter 28 he lays eyes on him for the first time: "Reality outran apprehension: Captain Ahab stood upon his quarter-deck."

There follows a remarkable three-paragraph description of Ahab's physical appearance in which Ishmael's (and the reader's) vague feelings of awe and apprehension are given a sharply detailed visual focus. "He looked," says Ishmael, "like a man cut away from the stake." The slender, lividly whitish scar that threads its way out from among his gray hairs and continues down "his tawny scorched face" until it disappears in his clothing is said to resemble a perpendicular gash caused by lightning in "the straight, lofty trunk of a great tree." So arresting is Ahab's scar that Ishmael does not immediately notice that much of his overbearing grimness is owing to "the barbaric white leg on which he partly stood." But it is Ahab's countenance more than anything else that compels attention. There is "an infinity of firmest fortitude, a determinate, unsurrenderable wilfulness" in his glance. But, as with Milton's Satan, there is also a "moody stricken" look—"the nameless regal overbearing dignity of some mighty woe." In the boldest figure used in Ishmael's description, there is "a crucifixion in his face."

In the next chapter Ahab is still presented strictly from the out-side. A brief conversation between him and Stubb, in which the overmastering force of Ahab's personality is instanced, is reported in its entirety. Additional secondhand information is provided through Stubb's recollection of what the Dough-Boy (the ship's steward) has told him of the disordered state in which he finds Ahab's hammock clothes, sheets, covers, and pillows each morn-ing. In chapter 30 the outside view of Ahab begins to be supple-mented by information from within. When Stubb leaves him, Ahab calls for his pipe and stool, sits on the weather side of the deck and smokes—at first in silence, but after a time Ishmael reports that "he soliloquized at last." At this point, one could assume that Ish-mael is using the word *soliloquy* loosely and that Ahab spoke to himself out loud in a way that could be heard by those near him. But it is nonetheless clear that the characterization of Ahab is mov-ing from an outside to an inside view and that Ishmael has taken a step in the direction of employing the narratorial device of psy-chological omniscience. The reader's sense of Ahab's character con-veyed by his physical description is supplemented and deepened by overhearing him wonder why smoking no longer soothes him. He decides it is because the pipe "is meant for sereneness" and the vapors it sends up are for "mild white hairs," not for his "torn, iron-grey locks." This brief chapter ends with Ahab tossing his still lighted pipe in the sea. It is the first but not the last time in *Moby-Dick* that we see him acting out his sense of isolated self-sufficiency by rejecting the dependent comforts of something—to recall the phrase Ishmael uses in the "The Lee Shore"—that's kind to our mortalities.

Chapter 33 ("The Specksynder") includes narratorial comment on the masterly way in which Ahab employs "the forms and usages of the sea" to his advantage in his dealings with his crew. Some of the comment is psychologically omniscient, as in the rather pon-derous observation that a certain previously unmanifested "sultan-ism" of Ahab's brain has become "incarnate in an irresistible dictatorship." Of itself, the psychological detail in this chapter is unimportant; but it does help to set the stage for the great scene in "The Quarter-Deck" (chap. 36), in which Ahab's powers over his

Ahab is dominating

crew are shown in a strictly dramatic fashion, the narrative point of view being that of a spectator in a theater whose knowledge of the characters on stage is restricted to what they say and do in the presence of other characters. The notation in the scene is superb: Ahab's "lowly humming to himself" while he waits for a hammer with which to nail the gold doubloon to the mainmast, "a sound so strangely muffled and inarticulate that it seemed the mechanical humming of the wheels of his vitality in him"; the sailors beginning "to gaze curiously at each other, as if marvelling how it was that they themselves [have become] so excited" by the seemingly purposeless questions Ahab has begun to ask them; and the telling deployment of Starbuck as foil to Ahab. It is in this scene that Ahab announces the real purpose of the *Pequod*'s voyage: to avenge himself on Moby Dick, the great white whale who has stripped him of his leg. When Starbuck cries out that such vengeance is blasphemous, Ahab answers with a powerful speech that may be regarded as a philosophical explanation of his quest. The white whale, he says, is but a mask (a symbol) of "some unknown but still reasoning thing." If a man is to strike at the "inscrutable malice" of this "inscrutable thing," he must "strike through the mask." "Talk not to me of blasphemy, man," Ahab tells his first mate, "I'd strike the sun itself if it insulted me." Ahab then orders each member of the crew to drink deep from the "brimming pewter," a demonic ritual of initiation that concludes with the pagan harpooneers drinking "the fiery waters" from the sockets of their harpoons. By the end of the scene Starbuck, like the two other mates, has "quailed before [Ahab's] strong, sustained, and mystic aspect."

After leaving the quarterdeck, Ahab retires to his cabin, where he is found in the next chapter ("Sunset"), which consists of the soliloquy he speaks as he gazes out of the cabin's stern windows and watches the sun go down. The change in mood and energy level from the previous chapter is striking, as is the change in Ahab's self-analysis. The literary historical overtones are correspondingly different. While Ahab's soliloquy contains several echoes of Satan's in *Paradise Lost*, it is less the Satan who echoes his Shakespearean antecedents than the Satan whose linear descendants include the dark Romantic hero—Manfred, for example,

who in Byron's drama also addresses a soliloquy to the setting sun
and who repeatedly describes himself as cut off from nature and
from the possibility of human or natural comforters. In "Sunset,"
Ahab's self-analysis is not philosophical but psychological. He reflects that "time was" when he was in vital contact with the natural
world: "as the sunrise nobly spurred me, so the sunset soothed."
But this is no longer the case. Like the Coleridge of the "Dejection"
ode or Matthew Arnold's Empedocles, Ahab has lost "the low, en-
joying power" because of the overcultivation of his gifts of "high
perception" (i.e., speculation). In this hell of Romantic self-consciousness, he has lost the power to feel one with the natural
world; as a result "this lovely light, it lights not me; all loveliness
is anguish to me, since I can ne'er enjoy." What Ahab is left to
follow is the unnatural, destructive path to his final purpose, which
(in his forbiddingly unnatural image of the railroad) "is laid with
iron rails, whereon my soul is grooved to run." The self-analysis in
"Sunset" would seem to offer a deeper diagnosis of Ahab's condition than that of "The Quarter-Deck," for it does not simply describe Ahab's present state; it also adumbrates an explanation of
how he came to be that way. At the same time it might also be
thought to imply at least a theoretical prescription: a way out of
Ahab's psychological state would be through the recovery of the
ability to feel part of the human and natural world. (As we shall
see, this possibility will be poignantly tested hundreds of pages later in "The Symphony.")

    In chapters 41 ("Moby Dick") and 44 ("The Chart") Ishmael
fully employs the novelistic device of psychological omniscience in
describing what makes Ahab hum. The result is a much more extended and complex analysis of his character than that provided in
"Sunset." Before considering this analysis it will be useful to bring
together the few pieces of information about Ahab's past that are
found elsewhere in *Moby-Dick* and arrange them according to his
chronology. (Since the sources of some of the information are not
authoritative the assembled data should be called the biographical
legend of Ahab.) In the Old Testament, Ahab, the husband of Jeze-
bel, is said to have done "evil in the sight of the Lord above all that
were before him" (1 Kings 16:30). But the captain of the *Pequod*

did not name himself. Peleg reports in chapter 16 that "'Twas a foolish, ignorant whim of his crazy, widowed mother, who died when he was only a twelvemonth old." Ahab, then, is an orphan. He went to sea at an early age and was only eighteen when as "a boy-harpooneer" he struck his first whale (chap. 132). Ahab says that this occurred "forty years ago," which would suggest that in the present time of the narrative he is in his late fifties. This seems right: while Ahab is repeatedly described as being old, he still possesses considerable stamina and strength, and his mental faculties are, if anything, all too sharp. At some point "long ago," so Elijah reports in chapter 19, something happened to Ahab off Cape Horn—presumably some sort of fit—as a result of which he "lay like dead for three days and nights." Equally portentous are the two other pieces of information about Ahab's past provided by Elijah: that he once fought "a deadly skrimmage with the Spaniard afore the altar in Santa" (a seaport in Peru) and that he spat into "the silver calabash." In the more recent past, Ahab, by now "past fifty," wedded a "young girl-wife" and sailed for Cape Horn the next day, leaving, as he puts it, "but one dent in my marriage pillow" (chap. 132). From this or a subsequent coupling a child was born. Even more recently, on his previous voyage Ahab lost a leg in attempting to kill Moby Dick. On the voyage back to Nantucket, Peleg reports that Ahab was "a little out of his mind for a spell" owing to "the sharp shooting pains in his bleeding stump." Ever since then, Peleg continues, Ahab has been "moody—desperate moody, and savage sometimes; but that will all pass off" (chap. 16). Peleg might not have spoken so optimistically, however, if he had known what is later revealed by the narrator in chapter 106: that not long prior to the *Pequod*'s sailing from Nantucket, Ahab had been found one night lying insensible on the ground, that his ivory limb had somehow been violently displaced and "all but pierced his groin," and that only with extreme difficulty was "the agonizing wound" entirely cured.

The key to the analysis of Ahab offered by the omniscient narrator in chapters 41 and 44 is the notion of monomania. A description of its effect on a person was included in an opinion written by Chief Justice Lemuel Shaw of the Supreme Judicial Court of Massachusetts in 1844 (three years before he would become the father-in-law of Herman Melville): "The conduct may be in some respects regular, the mind acute, and the conduct apparently governed by rules of propriety, and at the same time there may be insane delusion, by which the mind is perverted . . . the mind broods over *one idea* and cannot be reasoned out of it."[77] Such is the case with Ahab. Since his almost fatal encounter with Moby Dick he has come to cherish "a wild vindictiveness against the whale" and "in his frantic morbidness" has come to identify with him "not only all his bodily woes, but all his intellectual and spiritual exasperations." The white whale swims before him "as the monomaniac incarnation of all those malicious agencies which some deep men feel eating in them"; "all the subtle demonisms of life and thought; all evil" is to Ahab "visibly personified, and made practically assailable in Moby Dick." This obsession does not, however, enfeeble Ahab. Not one jot of his great natural intellect perishes in his broad madness; the "special lunacy" that commands "his general sanity" rather gives Ahab an awesome strength, " a thousand fold more potency than ever he had sanely brought to bear upon any one reasonable object."

This diagnosis is eloquent, detailed, and on its own terms convincing—even though the narrator makes no attempt to substantiate his important claim that "intellectual and spiritual exasperations" began to accumulate in Ahab before his first encounter with Moby Dick (one has only Elijah's dubious reference to a struggle at a Peruvian altar and the desecration of a silver calabash). Upon reflection, however, one might come to feel that the diagnosis is rather too clinical and that despite its greater complexity and apparent depth, it is essentially a more reductive and less profound analysis than the one that Ahab sketches in "Sunset." Certainly, Ishmael, the narrator of *Moby-Dick*, feels this way, for he no sooner concludes his diagnosis of monomania than he expresses dissatisfaction with it: "This is much; yet Ahab's larger, darker, deeper part remains unhinted." Ishmael attempts to supply some hints of this deeper part of Ahab through one of the most startling and puzzling images in *Moby-Dick*: "far down from within the very heart" of the grand and wonderful late Gothic Hotel de

Cluny in Paris lie the far more ancient ruins of a fourth-century
Roman palace, "those vast Roman halls of Thermes." Some persons, "ye nobler, sadder souls," must try to make their way down
to these halls, where "far beneath the fantastic towers of man's
upper earth, his root of grandeur, his whole awful essence" is
found. The visual representation of this essence is the sculpture of
a "captive king" with a broken throne "upholding on his frozen
brow the piled entablatures of ages." The "prouder, sadder souls"
who regard this "proud, sad king" notice a "family likeness! aye,
he did beget ye, ye young exiled royalties; and from your grim sire
only will the old State-secret come."

Compared to the vivid images used to describe Ahab's monomania, the meaning and import of the Hotel de Cluny image is
obscure—obscure but not opaque. It clearly has something to do
with loss—not the loss of a leg but a far more primal deprivation
that is closely connected with what later in *Moby-Dick* Ahab calls
"the secret of our paternity" (chap. 114). The image makes one
remember that Ahab was an orphan long before he was a hunter
of whales, a blasphemer, or a monomaniac. And it causes one to
reflect that whereas in "Sunset" Ahab had described the Romantic
predicament of his estrangement from the natural world, with
which he had once been in nourishing contact, what is suggested
here is that he suffers from a prior and more fundamental exile: he
is alienated from the deepest levels of his own being, from what
Ishmael in an analogous image at the end of chapter 41 calls "the
subterranean miner that works in us all," of whose presence we are
made aware only "by the ever shifting, muffled sound of his pick."
One further reflects that this estrangement would appear incapable
of remedy; if "the old State-secret" can only come from the stone
likeness of "your grim sire," it is presumably not going to come at
all.

A different image is used to convey something of the same import twenty-nine chapters later in the next inside view of Ahab that
Ishmael offers, a view provided not by narratorial omniscience but
through the dramatic device of the soliloquy. In chapter 70 ("The
Sphynx"), Ahab addresses the great black head of the decapitated
sperm whale that hangs from the *Pequod*'s side. "Speak, thou vast

and venerable head," he mutters, "and tell us the secret thing that is in thee. Of all divers, thou hast dived the deepest." The whale's head, he continues, knows the secrets of the ocean's depths, "that awful water-land," which is his "most familiar home." But though the head has seen all the wonders and horrors of the unknown life below, "not one syllable" does he utter; he can tell Ahab nothing. The geographical image of ocean depths unfathomable by humans is of course a refiguring of the architectural image of the ancient ruins far beneath the towers of the upper earth and the geological image of the subterranean miner. The one spiritual or psychological fact to which these natural facts are analogously linked is that there are areas within the individual—inner depths—that can never be known.

After "The Sphynx" one sees relatively little of Ahab for the next thirty-five chapters; when he does appear, as in the nicely described scene on the English whaling ship where he meets the good-natured Captain Boomer and the foppish Dr. Bunger, the reader's knowledge of his inner being is not increased. But from the beginning of the concluding movement of *Moby-Dick* in chapter 106, Ishmael the narrator, who had figured largely in the predominantly descriptive and discursive middle section of the book, recedes. Ahab becomes the dominant presence, as the *Pequod*, driven by his inflexible will, moves ever closer to its climactic encounter with Moby Dick. In these closing chapters, some use is made of psychological omniscience, but Ishmael mainly eschews this narratorial device in favor of the more immediate and engaging devices of soliloquy and dramatic scene, some of which, owing to Ahab's own sense of the theatrical, take on a heightened ritual or symbolic quality.

Chapters 106 to 109 ("Ahab's Leg," "The Carpenter," "Ahab and the Carpenter," and "Ahab and Starbuck in the Cabin") form a loose sequence. In the first of them one finds Ahab thinking about differences between "earthly felicities" and "heart-woes" in a way that recalls the figure of the "captive king" in the Hotel de Cluny image. While earthly felicities, even "the haymaking suns, and soft-cymballing, round harvest-moons," ever have "a certain unsignifying pettiness lurking in them," all heart-woes at bottom have "a mystic significance" and sometimes "an archangelic gran-deur." In tracing the "genealogies" of these high mortal miseries, meditation finally carries one back to the "sourceless primogeni-tures of the gods," who are to the race what the father is to the child. Once arrived at the source or root of what makes us what we are, we "must needs" realize that "the gods themselves are not for ever glad" and that the determining genetic inheritance is woe: "The ineffaceable, sad birth-mark on the brow of man, is but the stamp of sorrow in the signers."

Most of the sequence, however, is devoted not to a diagnosis of Ahab's psychological condition but to a much simpler and more straightforward description of one symptom of his condition: his hubristic self-sufficiency. Because Ahab needs a new ivory leg he summons the carpenter of the *Pequod*. A character sketch in chap-ter 107 of this previously unintroduced member of the crew pre-sents him as one of the mass of humanity, stolid, unreflective, unreasoning, "living without premeditated reference to this world or the next." In the scene between them in the following chapter Ahab does not fail to notice these qualities in the carpenter, nor to play up the symbolic suggestiveness of his dependence on such an unexceptional specimen: "Here I am," he exclaims with a self-dramatizing Byronic flourish, "proud as a Greek god, and yet standing debtor to this blockhead for a bone to stand on! Cursed be that mortal inter-indebtedness which will not do away with ledgers. I would be free as air; and I'm down in the whole world's [account] books." Ahab does not throw the carpenter overboard, as he does his pipe in chapter 30; but in the closing section of *Moby-Dick* he finds other situations through which to enact his obsessive need for self-sufficiency and give expression to his sense of superiority. In chapter 118, for example, he smashes his quad-rant and curses it as a "Foolish toy! babies' plaything." And in chapter 124, when Ahab fixes the compass that has become re-versed in an electrical storm he proclaims to his crew: "Look ye, for yourselves, if Ahab be not lord of the level loadstone!" Lest the reader has missed the point Ishmael concludes the chapter with a summary of what one has been shown. "In his fiery eyes of scorn and triumph, you then saw Ahab in all his fatal pride."

In two other late chapters Ahab is made to act out his heroic
defiance and godlike self-sufficiency in ways that might be described as more operatic than dramatic—more Wagnerian than
Shakespearean. In "The Forge" (chap. 113) he uses the blood of
his pagan harpooneers to temper the barbs of a newly made harpoon, while howling "deliriously" that he baptizes them not in the
name of God the Father but in the name of the devil. The other
chapter is 119 ("The Candles"), the spectacular typhoon scene during which the masts and yardarms of the *Pequod* become tipped
with the pallid fire of the corposants. The climax of the chapter is
Ahab's speech to the "clear spirit of clear fire." The principal import of his utterance, which recalls that of his speech to the crew
in "The Quarter-Deck," is defiant worship of the "speechless,
placeless power" of the fire and of the "unsuffusing thing beyond
thee." But perhaps the most interesting and suggestive moment in
Ahab's address is when he speaks of his kinship with the fire: "Now
I do glory in my genealogy. But thou art but my fiery father; my
sweet mother I know not. Oh cruel! what hast thou done with her."
At one level, the "sweet mother" may be thought to refer to the
benign aspect of the natural world, with which (vide the "Sunset"
chapter) Ahab feels no longer in contact. But at another and deeper
level the image of genealogy recalls the passage in "Ahab's Leg"
about the sad birthmark ineffaceably stamped on the human brow;
and the reference to the unknown sweet mother inevitably recalls
the fact that Ahab was an orphan and reminds one of the imagery
of primal exile in the Hotel de Cluny passage.

While a number of chapters in the closing section of *Moby-Dick*
seem to suggest that Ahab is now totally in the grip of his monomania and its attendant hubris, other scenes would seem to confirm Captain Peleg's observation in chapter 16: "striken, blasted,
if he be, Ahab has his humanities." One function of these scenes is
to increase suspense, for they raise the possibility that even at the
eleventh hour Ahab may become deflected from his destructive
purpose. But the scenes do more than simply add spice to the narrative; they also show that at some level of his being Ahab can still
be moved by human and natural emotions, that he is not a man
who has "no heart at all," as he says he wishes to be in chapter

108. The scenes also add a poignancy and a deeply affecting quality to the reader's response to Ahab. One example is the loving relationship that is shown to have developed between Ahab and Pip, the black boy who has lost his mind through a too direct exposure to the empty immensities of midocean. "Here boy," says the captain to Pip in chapter 125, "Ahab's cabin shall be Pip's home henceforth. . . . Thou touchest my inmost centre, boy; thou art tied to me by cords woven of my heart-strings." It is clear that Ahab is partly drawn to Pip because he sees in the boy's madness a reflection of his own. But in Pip, unlike the doubloon, Ahab sees more than an image of himself. He also sees another maimed human being and feels a reciprocal pull: for while Ahab ministers to Pip, he comes to realize that at the same time Pip is ministering to him. "There is that in thee, poor lad," he tells him in chapter 129, "which I feel too curing to my malady. . . . If thou speakest thus to me more, Ahab's purpose keels up in him."

While looking into Starbuck's eyes in the magnificent chapter "The Symphony" (chap. 132), Ahab is even more strongly drawn out from the contracting circle of his monomania. The natural setting of this chapter is an exceptionally beautiful morning in which the elements seem lovingly combined and interdependent; air and sea are hardly separable in the "all-pervading azure" of the "clear steel-blue day"; the "feminine air" and the "masculine sea" seem to respond to each other "even as bride and groom." As Ahab gazes on the scene its loveliness seems "to dispel . . . the cankerous thing in his soul." The glad, happy air and winsome sky "did at last stroke and caress him; the step-mother world, so long cruel" seems to throw affectionate arms around him. Finally, "from beneath his slouched hat, Ahab dropped a tear into the sea." The day revives his tenderest memories, and when he begins to speak of them to his first mate, Ahab is at his most sympathetic. He gazes into Starbuck's eye, not because he sees any answering madness there but because there is in that "magic glass," as he calls it, an image of the green land, the bright hearthstone, and his own wife and child. Like the reader, Starbuck is deeply moved. He asks Ahab why anyone would want to hunt the hated fish and urges him to "fly these deadly waters! let us home!" But when he next looks up at his captain what he sees is chilling: "Ahab's glance was averted; like a blighted fruit tree he shook, and cast his last, cindered apple to the soil." When he speaks—as much to himself as to Starbuck— it is only to give voice to his irremissive exasperation of spirit. He speaks of the "nameless, inscrutable, unearthly thing" that compels him on to his destruction "against all natural lovings and longings [of] my own proper, natural heart."

The next day the great white whale is finally sighted. Two days later Ahab, Starbuck, Pip, and all save one of the *Pequod*'s crew are dead. Ahab remains heroically but ineffectually defiant to the end. On the second day of the chase he again speaks tenderly to Starbuck and alludes to the scene between them in "The Symphony": "that hour we both saw—thou know'st what, in one another's eyes." And he once again uses the concept of fate to explain why he cannot act otherwise than he does: "The whole act's immutably decreed. . . . I am the Fates' lieutenant. I act under orders." For the reader who has given careful attention to the presentation of Ahab throughout *Moby-Dick*, particularly to the inside views provided by narratorial omniscience and soliloquy, the concept of an external fate will hardly seem a satisfactory explanation of what makes Ahab Ahab. Whether the cause is monomania, a split between the inner world of self and the outer natural world, or is rooted in a primal dispossession and exile from the deepest sources of his inner being, it is a psychological rather than a superhuman cause. Which of these internal conditions one considers predominant will have an important bearing on the questions of how representative of the human condition Captain Ahab is and whether there is any less destructive alternative that does not require remaining a provincial and sentimentalist in Truth. In exploring these questions we must first consider the other characters in *Moby-Dick* (and their characterization) and then attempt a comparison of the inner being and the vision of the work's two dominant presences—Ahab and Ishmael the narrator.

VIII: Starbuck and Others

> I have written a wicked book, and feel spotless as the lamb.
>
> *Melville, letter to Hawthorne*

In his discussion of original characters in fiction, the narrator of *The Confidence-Man* insists that just as there can be "but one planet to one orbit, so there can be but one . . . original character to one work of invention." But he goes on to say that "for new, singular, striking, odd, eccentric and all sorts of entertaining and instructive characters, a good fiction may be full of them."[78] *Moby-Dick* is not such a fiction. It is not a novel à la Dickens or Thackeray. Because of its subject and setting (hunting whales in mid-ocean), its cast of characters is severely limited in number and occupation and is further restricted to a single sex. And because of the thematic urgencies of the narrator, the principal supporting players are all stylized and schematized. They are not rounded characters and they do not change. They are rather representative of different states of intellectual and spiritual being.

One of these characters is purely emblematic. When Fedallah is first seen on the deck of the *Pequod* in chapter 48 ("The First Lowering") a brief but sharply etched description of his appearance is provided: rumpled Chinese jacket of black cotton, wide trousers of the same color, glistening white plaited turban, and "one white tooth evilly protruding from [his] steel-like lips." But the clothing that principally interests Ishmael is the portentous symbolic drapings with which Fedallah is invested at the end of chapter 50—that aura of "muffled mystery," the factitious quality of which we have already noted. The association of Fedallah with "the ghostly aboriginalness of earth's primal generations" does not involve the use of psychological omniscience, the narratorial tool that Ishmael elsewhere uses so superbly. It is simply a fuzzy symbolic overlay that supplies one pole—the dark, evil one—toward which Ahab is shown to be drawn in the closing sections of *Moby-Dick* as he moves away from the pole of goodness and humanity represented in their different ways by Pip and Starbuck. (At the same time, the Ahab-Fedallah duo also provides a thematic counterweight to the much more interesting Ishmael-Queequeg relationship.)

Fedallah is part of the iconography of several tableaulike scenes. At the end of chapter 73, as he examines the head of a decapitated right whale and compares its deep wrinkles to the lines on his own hand, "Ahab chanced so to stand, that the Parsee [Fedallah] occupied his shadow; while, if the Parsee's shadow was there at all it served only to blend with, and lengthen Ahab's." The Parsees are an Indian religious sect of Persian and Zoroastrian origin, who hold a Manichean belief in the divine warfare of good and evil and who are drawn to the worship of fire. Not for nothing, then, does Fedallah later kneel in front of Ahab, who puts his foot on the Parsee while he stands before the fire of the corposants to address "the clear spirit of clear fire, whom on these seas I as Persian once did worship" (chap. 119). In another scene Fedallah is again found kneeling before Ahab, who is looking up toward the sun (fire) and deciding to smash the quadrant. When Starbuck turns away "with despair" from Ahab at the end of "The Symphony" it is Fedallah's eyes, rather than the first mate's, that Ahab finds himself gazing into. In the last chapter of *Moby-Dick*, eye contact is made between the two for the last time as, pinioned by tangled ropes to the back of Moby Dick, " the half torn body of the Parsee was seen; his subtle raiment frayed to shreds; his distended eyes turned full upon old Ahab" (chap. 135).

It is a riveting moment, which is no less compelling for being so extravagantly emblematic. In retrospect, however, the reflective reader might wonder what difference it would make if all of Fedallah's appearances were expunged from the text of *Moby-Dick*. The answer is that while a darkly lurid tinge would be missing from certain scenes, and a frisson or two sacrificed, nothing of real importance would be lost. The depiction of Ahab's inner being would be unaffected; and his psychological complexity might even be more clearly seen once the invitation to reductive generalizations about a cosmic struggle between good and evil was no longer in the text.

Pip appears in *Moby-Dick* just as infrequently as Fedallah, but he is a more interesting character and plays a richer and more suggestive role. In the closing section of the book there is the important interaction between Pip and Ahab, a reciprocal pull quite unlike the static Ahab-Fedallah blocking. And Pip is a much more interesting and complex characterization in his own right. No muffled mythic trappings are applied to his outside; psychological omniscience is used to give the reader an extended inside view of how and why he lost his mind. This analysis in turn suggests correspondences and contrasts between Pip's state of being and those of Ahab and Ishmael, and throws an interesting light on both, particularly the latter.

The key chapter concerning Pip is "The Castaway" (chap. 93), which describes how he came to lose his sense of individual identity. At the beginning of the chapter Pip is described as a "tender-hearted" boy who "loved life, and all life's peaceable securities." Back home in Connecticut, he and his tambourine had enlivened "many a fiddler's frolic on the green; and at melodious even-tide" he had even been able to make the natural world appear to wear the colors of his own spirit, as with his "gay ha-ha!" he had turned "the round horizon into one star-belled tambourine." Pip's natural element is—to borrow Ahab's terms—that of earthly felicities. But his being cannot withstand the shock of transition from them to the heart-woes of midocean. When for the second time he panics and jumps from Stubb's boat, Pip is left behind "like a hurried traveller's trunk," and becomes a "lonely castaway" floating on the empty expanse of the shoreless ocean. The "awful loneliness" becomes "intolerable" to Pip: "the intense concentration of self in the middle of such a heartless immensity, my God! who can tell it?"

The clear echo here is to the climax of Ishmael's meditation in "The Whiteness of the Whale," when he speaks of "the heartless voids and immensities of the universe" that stab us "from behind with thoughts of annihilation" (chap. 42). Like Ishmael in the epilogue, Pip is rescued by the merest chance. But "from that hour the little negro went about the deck an idiot; such, at least, they said he was. The sea had jeeringly kept his finite body up, but drowned the infinite of the soul." One is again reminded of Ishmael, this time of the loss of the sense of individual identity that attends his experiences of merging with the visible world, as described in "The Mast-Head" and elsewhere. But are we meant to think of these experiences as a form of insanity? And when it is said of Pip and his otherworldly wisdom that "He saw God's foot upon the treadle of the loom, and spoke [called to] it," one is reminded of two similar images used by Ishmael to describe a felt sense of universal oneness—in "The Mat-Maker" (chap. 46) and in the description of the "wondrous sight" of the whale's skeleton bedecked with verdant foliage in "A Bower in the Arsacides" (chap. 102). But does the reminder serve to confirm, to qualify, or to undermine Ishmael's visions of cosmic felicity? And is it similarities or contrasts that one finds in comparing Pip's becoming a castaway to Ishmael's "like abandonment" in the epilogue, as the reader is explicitly invited to do in the last sentence of "The Castaway"?

On the schematic level, Queequeg is the opposite equal of Fedallah; but, like Pip, he is a more important presence in *Moby-Dick*. While the Parsee, Ahab's dark double, is the incarnation of a primeval darkness, Queequeg, the bosom friend of Ishmael, is the embodiment of a prelapsarian goodness, a noble savage who possesses the same naturally wholesome characteristics that Melville (or rather Tommo, the narrator of *Typee*, Melville's first book) found in the cannibal savages of an island of the Marquesas. Tommo had been surprised to find in the Typees "an inherent principle of honesty and charity towards each other" as well as an "indwelling . . . universally diffused perception of what is *just* and *noble*." These cannibal savages dealt "more kindly with each other, and [seemed] more humane" than occidental students of morality or pious Christians. In observing their "thoughtless happiness" Tommo did not even distinctly identify "the love of kindred . . . for it seemed blended in the general love."[79] It is to the same qualities in Queequeg that Ishmael begins to feel himself "mysteriously," perhaps even homoerotically, drawn during their time as bedmates at the Spouter-Inn. "Christian kindness," says Ishmael the character to himself, "has proved but hollow courtesy," and he will therefore try the pagan friend who stirs "strange feelings" in him and who is even said—in a striking appropriation of a term with unmistakably Christian overtones—to have "redeemed" him (chap. 10).

Ishmael describes his new friend's manner of being in the world as a state of "unconsciousness," by which he means a lack of self-consciousness (chap. 13). Because of the unreflective simplicity of Queequeg's being there is no reason for Ishmael the narrator to offer inside views of him. Queequeg is frequently present in the early chapters, and he is always seen from the outside in relation to either Ishmael or other members of civilized, Christian society. The results of these encounters of savage and civilized are entertaining, as in Ishmael's droll description of his first meeting with Queequeg in the bedroom of the Spouter-Inn or the later scene in Mrs. Hussey's Nantucket boardinghouse in chapter 17 in which Ishmael breaks down a bedroom door in order to see what has become of his friend, only to find him coolly squatting on his hams in the middle of the room, holding his black idol Yojo on top of his head. Sometimes the result of these encounters points a moral as well as entertains, as when Ishmael is led to make some ironic contrasts between civilization and savagery and between the Christian and pagan religions. In chapter 18, for example, there is a mixture of satire and entertainment when Captains Peleg and Bildad make an issue of the religious persuasion of Queequeg until he demonstrates his remarkable expertise with a harpoon, after which he is signed on with no further questions asked.

After the *Pequod* sails, the appearances of Queequeg become as infrequent as those of Ishmael the character, in whose company he is usually found when he does appear. As we have seen, in "The Mat-Maker" and "The Monkey-Rope" the dominant mood is a warm and pliant general love that recalls their cosy "hearts' honeymoon" in the Spouter-Inn (chap. 10). But as earthly felicities become ever more recessive on the *Pequod,* and the heart-woes of Ahab more dominant, so Queequeg is seen less and less. He does not lose his mind, as does Pip, but he does have a peculiar fever that darkens his thoughts and causes him to order his coffin made. Since his "unconsciousness" cannot accommodate any degree of complexity, Queequeg is made to fade out of the closing section of *Moby-Dick.* His place is taken by his coffin, which becomes a more versatile artifact of more complex significance—a coffin life buoy. On the last page of the book, it is to the floating coffin rather than to his comrade that Ishmael clings in order to be saved.

Two of the mates on the *Pequod* figure importantly in *Moby-*

Dick: Stubb, the second mate, and Starbuck, the first. Together with Flask, the third mate, they are introduced in chapters 26 and 27 not dramatically but through character sketches that contain in embryo almost everything that the reader needs to know or comes to learn about them. Each mate is shown to represent a different position on the intellectual and spiritual spectrum. Together with Pip they provide an important part of the background and the context for thinking about and assessing the positions occupied by Ahab and the two Ishmaels. Flask is far and away the least interesting of the three, because he is almost totally unimaginative and unreflective. In the thumbnail sketch offered in chapter 27 he is said to be "so utterly lost . . . to all sense of reverence for the many marvels" of whales that he considers them "but a species of magnified mouse, or . . . water-rat." His unimaginativeness does not stand in the way of his occasionally providing lighter moments during the voyage, as in the description in chapter 34 of his discomfiture while at dinner at Ahab's cabin table. In chapter 81, however, his cruel pricking of the strangely discolored protuberance the size of a bushel on the flank of an old, blind whale is no laughing matter. It is rather an indication of his lack of reverence for whales in particular and of his "pervading mediocrity" (chap. 41) in general. The latter quality is further instanced in his unimaginative meditation on the doubloon—he wonders only about the number of cigars it will buy. And even at the moment of his death, the only significance he can find in the *Pequod*'s fatal encounter with Moby Dick is also monetary—the comparatively "few coppers" that will come to his mother because of the premature termination of the voyage (chap. 135).

Stubb is a much more colorful and engaging character. In his introductory sketch in chapter 27 he is described as "a happy-go-lucky; neither craven nor valiant. . . . Good-humored, easy, and careless . . . an easy-going, unfearing man." Stubb presides over his whale boat "as if the most deadly encounter were but a dinner, and his crew all invited guests," and is as particular about the comfortable arrangement of his part of the boat "as an old stage-driver is about the snugness of his box." He handles his lance "as cooly and offhandedly as a whistling tinker his hammer," and even "hums old rigadig tunes" while at his perilous work. His most significant physical characteristic—indeed his visual leitmotiv—is his short black pipe, which is "one of the regular features of his face. You would as soon have expected him to turn out of his bunk without his nose as without his pipe." As with Dickens's humorous characters, Stubb is mainly brought to life through his distinctive speech, which is at its most flavorful and pungent in his exordia to his boat crew: "The devil fetch ye, ye ragamuffin rapscallions; ye are all asleep. Stop snoring, ye sleepers and pull. . . . Why in the name of gudgeons and ginger-cakes don't ye pull?" (chap. 48); "Start her, Tash, my boy—start her, all; but keep cool, keep cool— cucumbers is the word—easy, easy" (chap. 61); "Don't be afraid, my butter-boxes, ye'll be picked up presently—all right—I saw some sharks astern—St. Bernard's dogs, you know—relieve distressed travellers" (chap. 81).

In the long middle section of *Moby-Dick* a number of scenes in which Stubb dominates provide comic relief similar in its broad humor to that offered by Queequeg's encounters with civilized Christians in the early chapters of the book. Examples are found in the second mate's droll exchanges with Fleece the cook in "Stubb's Supper" (chap. 64) and in the account of how he duped the French captain in "The Pequod Meets the Rose-Bud" (chap. 91). But the more important and more interesting function of Stubb concerns the position he occupies in the spiritual and philosophical spectrum of *Moby-Dick*. Compared to Flask, Stubb does have some capacity to be moved by what is outside of himself. Since he can dream, as we know from "Queen Mab" (chap. 31), he can in his way respond imaginatively to events. He is also responsive enough to admire Ahab (chap. 118) and to be awed by the fire of the corposants (chap. 119). In the closing section of the book, he is sensitive enough to the mood of the *Pequod* to have a premonition of disaster and even to see a symbolic meaning in the lashing down of the ship's anchors (chap. 121). And if at the moment of his death his thoughts do not turn to speculative considerations (as do Ahab's and Starbuck's) at least he thinks of something more vital than money. As we know from his last words, Stubb goes to his watery death with the body of a young woman on his mind: "cherries! cherries! cherries! Oh, Flask, for one red cherry ere we die" (chap. 135).

Unlike Flask and Queequeg, Stubb even has enough inner life to be given a soliloquy or two through which his philosophy of life is directly presented to the reader. The most important of them is the first, which fills the one paragraph of "First Night-Watch" (chap. 39) and gives the second mate's reaction to "The Quarter-Deck" scene. "I've been thinking over it ever since, and that ha, ha's the final consequence. Why so? Because a laugh's the wisest, easiest answer to all that's queer; and come what will, one comfort's always left—that unfailing comfort is, it's all predestinated, . . . I know not all that may be coming, but be it what it will, I'll go to it laughing." This belief in supernatural causation—in events being predetermined by some force above and beyond man—might seem to move Stubb close to the position occupied by Ahab on the spiritual spectrum of *Moby-Dick*. His speech could even be thought a demotic rescoring of Ahab's oft-repeated belief in the immutable decrees of fate, the only difference being that in the prescripted drama in which they are acting, Ahab plays a tragic role and Stubb a comic one. One might further reflect that Stubb's part is more sympathetic than Ahab's in that it does not involve the rejection of what's kind to our mortalities, does not cut one off from others, and allows one to live neither suicidally nor solipsistically.

This is not the view of the matter that Ahab has, however, nor the view that the reader of *Moby-Dick* is invited to have. Both Ahab and Ishmael the narrator would agree with the Socratic dictum that the unexamined life is not worth living. Ahab's dismissive judgment of Stubb is that he is "brave as fearless fire (and as mechanical)" (chap. 133); and Ishmael earlier strikes a similar note in speaking of his "invulnerable jollity of indifference and recklessness" (chap. 41). Stubb is invulnerable and indifferent because he does not think. His belief that "it's all predestinated" is not the result of reflection, but a substitute for reflection—a pat formula that allows Stubb to be programmatically brave and metronomically cheerful. This is the reason psychological omniscience is never used in his presentation. In chapter 27, when he is first described to the reader, Ishmael remarks that "what he thought of death it-self, there is no telling." There is no telling not because Ishmael's narratorial powers fail him when he comes to the *Pequod*'s second mate, but because there is nothing to tell. Stubb has no inner life. As we have seen, he can in his way respond imaginatively to nat-ural facts but never to the extent that he is teased into thought and speculation.

While it is hard not to agree with Ahab's scornful dismissal of Stubb's mechanical nature, it is more difficult, at least initially, to agree with his insistence that the second mate and the first are op-posite equals: that "Starbuck is Stubb reversed, and Stubb is Star-buck; and ye two are all mankind" (chap. 133). Starbuck is, after Ahab and Ishmael, the most important character in *Moby-Dick* and the richest characterization in terms of both psychological depth and thematic implication. The most important single fact about Starbuck is that he is a Christian. This brings up an impor-tant subject for critical consideration: whether and to what extent *Moby-Dick* either endorses, qualifies, criticizes, pulverizes, or is antagonistic to Christian beliefs. Before looking at Starbuck in de-tail, therefore, the opportunity should now be taken to examine the places in the book where Christians or Christian beliefs are described, presented, or commented on.

Queequeg's presence in the early chapters leads to a certain amount of satirical observation or implied ironic comment on New England Christianity. It is not easy, however, to take these enter-taining remarks as seriously as some commentators do. One un-derstands, of course, that Ishmael's tongue is in his cheek when he refers to "we good Presbyterian Christians" (chap. 17); and it is equally hard to miss the point of the observation that Captain Bil-dad has long since "come to the sage and sensible conclusion that a man's religion is one thing, and this practical world quite anoth-er" (chap. 16). But such aperçus are no more telling about the Christian religion than Ishmael's crack that Queequeg's head re-sembles George Washington's—"cannibalistically developed"—is about American history (chap. 10). And there is nothing even va-guely satirical or critical in the touching description in chapter 22 of how the old salts Peleg and Bildad are affected when the moment comes for them to leave the outsetting *Pequod* and return to Nantucket harbor.

Ishmael's visit to the Whaleman's Chapel in New Bedford, especially the sermon he hears by the celebrated Father Mapple, is much more important to a consideration of the Christian elements of *Moby-Dick*. Mapple's sermon in chapter 9 is one of the book's principal set pieces and according to some commentators it provides a prospective gloss for what subsequently happens, offering an interpretative key with which the reader can unlock the meaning of *Moby-Dick*. Such, for example, was the claim of W. H. Auden, who argued in an essay called "The Christian Tragic Hero" that *Moby-Dick* was a Christian tragedy of possibility rather than a Greek tragedy of necessity. More than once, Auden claimed, Ahab is offered the possibility to choose to do otherwise than he does. Because he is of heroic stature, much is demanded of him; the ultimate requirement "is stated in Father Mapple's sermon, and it is to become a saint—i.e., the individual who of his own free will surrenders his will to the will of God."[80]

Auden might have embarrassed himself less if he had realized that Father Mapple's sermon contains a "two-stranded lesson" (as Mapple himself points out) and that surrender to the will of God is only the first of them. This part of the sermon retells and elaborates the Old Testament story of Jonah and the Whale in order to draw out "a lesson to us all as sinful men." The climax of this first strand comes when Jonah learns the orthodox Puritan lesson that salvation comes through faith rather than good works. He ceases to "weep and wail for direct deliverance. He feels that his dreadful punishment is just." This is "true and faithful repentance; not clamorous for pardon, but grateful for punishment." This lesson does indeed emphasize passive submission to the will of God, and it is equally true to say that it is a traditional Christian doctrine. It might even be considered the most distinctive Christian doctrine. At least this is what Ishmael the narrator suggests en passant in chapter 86 when he speaks of the divine love of the Son depicted in "the soft, curled, hermaphroditical" Christs of "Italian pictures": "destitute as they are of all brawniness, [they] hint nothing of any power, but the mere negative, feminine one of submission and endurance, which on all hands it is conceded, form the peculiar practical virtues of his teachings." But for Ishmael to say that "all hands" concede the centrality of this Christian doctrine is not to say that he considers that this "mere negative, feminine" tenet is a true, wise, or healthy belief, or that he in any way endorses it.

The second strand in Mapple's sermon, the other lesson, is addressed not to his congregation but "to me as a pilot of the living God." There is nothing passive, soft, or feminine about this "more awful lesson," which climaxes in an exultant spiritual warwhoop. "Woe to him who seeks to please rather than to appal!" cries out Mapple "with a heavenly enthusiasm." "Delight is to him [who] ever stands forth his own inexorable self . . . who gives no quarter in the truth, and kills, burns and destroys all sin though he pluck it out from under the robes of Senators and Judges." This lesson also adumbrates a Christian doctrine—the Puritan conception of the leader who consciously acts as the instrument of God. Once again, it is not at all clear that Ishmael in any way endorses this doctrine. How *could* someone like Ishmael, who knows that all beliefs—like all knowledge—are uncertain and problematic, and that there is inevitably a subjective element in all spiritual perception? As he remarks in chapter 17, "the reason why most dyspeptic religionists cherish such melancholy notions about their hereafters" is that "all thoughts born of a fast must necessarily be half-starved." Hell, he goes on, "is an idea first born on an undigested apple-dumpling."

The most famous literary dyspeptic of the nineteenth century was Thomas Carlyle, that Protestant-Romantic warrior whose verbal thunderclaps resemble those of Mapple and whom Matthew Arnold called a moral desperado.[81] Given the mature Ishmael's sense of the world, how can the Puritan hero celebrated by Mapple be called anything else? How could he be other than self-elected to his task by a prideful subjective impulse? Who in *Moby-Dick* resembles this spiritual hero? Captain Ahab, of course, for whose monomania the second strand of Mapple's sermon suggests a religiocultural source. Father Mapple's sermon is, then, like almost everything else in *Moby-Dick*, distinctly ambivalent in implication.

Far from offering a Christian interpretative key to the work, it might rather be thought to contain a two-stranded lesson in how not to do it.

After Ishmael leaves the Whaleman's Chapel, neither he nor his older, narratorial self again refer to either strand of Father Mapple's sermon. It is as if they have had no effect on him at all. The most basic reason is suggested by the other sermon preached in *Moby-Dick:* that of Fleece to the sharks in chapter 64 ("Stubb's Supper"). Stubb, who is feasting on the whale steak prepared for him by Fleece, urges the Negro cook to go to the side of the *Pequod* and preach to the sharks who are themselves feasting on the body of the dead whale attached to the ship:

> Your woraciousness, fellow-critters, I don't blame ye so much for; dat is natur, and can't be helped; but to gobern dat wicked natur, dat is de pint. You is sharks, sartin; but if you gobern de shark in you, why den you be angel; for all angel is not'ing more dan de shark well goberned. Now, look here, bred'ren, just try wonst to be cibil, a helping yourselbs from dat whale. Don't be tearin' de blubber out your neighbour's mout, I say. Is not one shark dood right as toder to dat whale? And, by Gor, non on you has de right to dat whale; dat whale belong to some one else.

The sermon is as broadly comic as the chapter that contains it. But if one stands back from the scene one can see a significant aspect to the burlesque. Not for nothing does Stubb cry out at the sermon's conclusion, "Well done, old Fleece! that's Christianity." What Fleece has described in his pungent vernacular is a version of the Christian world view of the Middle Ages and Renaissance, which held that man's place in the hierarchy of creation was higher than the animals' and the world of death and hell below, but lower than that of the angels and the empyrean of the Deity. Through grace and through the practice of the Christian virtues, one could hope to efface the traces of original sin within (to "gobern de shark in you") and to ascend rather than descend in the scale of creation. It is wholly appropriate that this Christian cosmology is ridiculed because, as we have seen, the worldview of *Moby-Dick* is Romantic, not Christian. Ishmael is committed to an in-out rather than an up-down premise, in which the two termini are not the Christian hell at one end and the Christian heaven at the other, but the ego on the one hand and everything that lies outside it on the other. Ishmael, then, never mentions Father Mapple's sermon because it is irrelevant to his concerns; he lives in a different world.

Starbuck is the exemplary Christian in *Moby-Dick*. He is first mentioned at the end of chapter 21 when a shipmate observes in passing that the first mate is a "good man, and a pious." The accuracy of this remark is confirmed in the character sketch offered in chapter 26 that uses psychological omniscience to probe the depths of Starbuck's inner life, A "staid, steadfast man" with a basic ruggedness in his nature, Starbuck possesses courage that is not the devil-may-care fearlessness of Stubb but a useful and practical commodity, one of "the great staple outfits of the ship, like her beef and her bread, and not to be foolishly wasted." Yet for all his "hardy sobriety and fortitude" Starbuck is for a seaman "unusually conscientious and [has] a deep natural reverence." It is not unusual that he is superstitious; what is out of the ordinary is that the "outward portents and inward presentiments" that are his seem "rather to spring, somehow, from intelligence than from ignorance." The "welded iron of his soul" is still further bent by "his faraway domestic memories of his young Cape wife and child" and his "terrible . . . remembrances" of the loss at sea of his own father and brother.

Ishmael's immediate purpose in pointing up these humane, softening qualities of Starbuck's nature is to explain at the outset how a man of such a strong character will so easily become subservient to Ahab's dark power. The key point is that Starbuck's courage is more a physical than a metaphysical quality; it "cannot withstand those more terrific, because more spiritual terrors, which sometimes menace you from the concentrating brow of an enraged and mighty man." The reason he cannot stand up to Ahab is not that Starbuck lacks the capacity for spiritual perception (as does Stubb, for example, who is similarly cowed). It is rather that Starbuck's vision is too land-based, too rooted in natural and domestic pieties and insufficiently tempered by exposure not to the physical but to the metaphysical perils of the ocean. To recall an image used else-where in *Moby-Dick*, Starbuck, unlike Ahab, has not pushed off from the green and insular Tahiti within and encountered the ter-rors of the half-known life.

The moment of "the fall of valor in the soul" of Starbuck, pre-dicted in chapter 27, occurs in the quarterdeck scene in chapter 36. It is Ahab who remarks the moment. Starbuck has instinctively cried out that the captain's plan to wreak "vengeance on a dumb brute" seems blasphemous. But like the rest of the crew he is si-lenced by Ahab's demonstration of his powers of spiritual percep-tion in his speech about visible objects being merely pasteboard masks. This speech ends with an aside in which Ahab notes that Starbuck has now become contaminated, and consequently inca-pacitated, by his own more powerful vision: "Something shot from my dilated nostrils, he has inhaled it in his lungs. Starbuck now is mine." The next person to speak in the scene is Starbuck, who murmurs lowly, "God keep me!—keep us all!"

In his soliloquy in chapter 38 ("Dusk") Starbuck struggles to understand what has happened to him on the quarterdeck. "My soul is more than matched," he reflects, "she's overmanned; and by a madman! . . . He drilled deep down, and blasted all my reason out of me! I think I see his impious end, but feel that I must help him to it." Starbuck goes on to console himself with the Christian hope that God may choose to thwart Ahab's blasphemous plan: "His heaven-insulting purpose, God may wedge aside." And at the end of his meditation the first mate again hitches his wagon to a Christian star: "Oh, life! 'tis in an hour like this, with soul beat down and held to knowledge,—as wild, untutored things are forced to feed—Oh, life! 'tis now that I do feel the latent horror in thee! but 'tis not me! that horror's out of me! and with the soft feeling of the human in me, yet will I try to fight ye, ye grim, phan-tom futures! Stand by me, hold me, bind me, O ye blessed influ-ences!" This passage deserves close attention. In it Starbuck seems poised on the brink of recognition of the "latent horror" of life, and ready to begin the passage from earthly felicities to heart-woes, from the insular Tahiti to the terrors of the half-known life, from all that's kind to our mortalities to the howling infinite. But at the last psychological moment, so to speak, Starbuck pulls back from this knowledge and denies that the horror of life has any essential connection with him: "that horror's out of me!" he insists. What Starbuck refuses to recognize is that the line between land and sea, blessed and blasphemous, loveliness and horror, does not run between humanity and nature or between people, but rather runs through each individual. Starbuck prefers to remain cocooned in "the soft feeling of the human in me" and since (as he himself recognizes) such softness can hardly prevail against "ye grim, phantom futures" he is forced to put his trust in a supernatural softness, in "ye blessed influences" above. Such a posture may be a version of Christian submissiveness to the will of God; but it is also an example of self-willed spiritual immaturity, of remaining a provincial and a sentimentalist in Truth.

Starbuck appears only intermittently and never for very long in the middle section of *Moby-Dick,* and when he does he is always in character. In chapter 41 the narrator sums up what the reader has already been both told and shown: that the crew of the *Pequod* is "morally enfeebled . . . by the incompetence of mere unaided virtue or right-mindedness in Starbuck." The first mate is predictably appalled by the "white ghost" of the giant squid in chapter 59; and in chapter 99, as we have seen, he furnishes a Christian interpretation of what is depicted on the doubloon. Starbuck's interpretation of Pip's madness in chapter 110 also shows his habitual desire to find a soft, supernatural meaning in natural facts. "So to my fond faith," he avers, "poor Pip, in this strange sweetness of his lunacy, brings heavenly vouchers of all our heavenly homes." Needless to say, this is hardly as penetrating or convincing an analysis as that supplied by Ishmael the narrator. Starbuck's symbolic perceptions in chapter 114 ("The Gilder") similarly point up his naive refusal to face the spiritual facts. Ahab's gazing out on the blessed calm of an exceptionally lovely day leads to his profound meditation on "the secret of our paternity." The same scene prompts in Starbuck's reverie only another example of his self-inflicted spiritual blindness, his refusal to acknowledge the horror in life. "Loveliness unfathomable," he says as he looks down at the surface of the golden sea, "Tell me not of thy teeth-tiered sharks, and thy kidnapping cannibal ways. Let faith oust fact: let fancy oust memory; I look deep down and do believe."

Starbuck's moral enfeeblement is again instanced in chapter 123 ("The Musket") in his agonized self-debate over whether to kill Ahab. And his soft human qualities are again instanced in the scene with Ahab in "The Symphony" (chap. 132). On the third day of the chase in chapter 135—the day of his death—Starbuck is at his most sympathetically moving as he describes his strange sense that his life's journey is coming to an end. "Future things swim before me, as in empty outlines and skeletons; all the past is somehow grown dim. Mary, girl! thou fadest in pale glories behind me; boy! I seem to see but thine eyes grown wondrous blue." At the climactic moment, Starbuck resolves to die like a man fighting to the last and seems momentarily to doubt the efficacy of his Christian beliefs: "Is this the end of all of my bursting prayers? all my life-long fidelities? . . . My God, stand by me now!" The answer is that yes, this is the end. In the Christian hymn sung by the congregation of the Whaleman's Chapel in chapter 9, the castaway, arched over by the ribs and terrors of the whale and plunging to despair, calls on his God, and is rescued from his black distress. But there is no such "Deliverer God" for Starbuck. And while there is much for the tender-minded to be moved by in his pathetic end, the tough-minded reader will recognize the truth of Ahab's remark about the similarity of Starbuck and Stubb. The difference between the latter's "ha" and the former's Christian God is one of degree only, not of kind. Both notions of a supernatural final consequence serve to release their believers from the burden of encountering, recognizing, and accepting into consciousness what the older Ishmael calls the knowledge of the demonism of the world. This is a burden that the older Ishmael and Ahab both carry. How they manage this burden and whether it is ultimately supportable are questions we must now consider.

IX: *Ishmael's Vision*

A loss of something ever felt I—
The first that I could recollect
Bereft I was—of what I knew not
Too young that any should suspect

A Mourner walked among the children
I notwithstanding went about
As one bemoaning a Dominion
Itself the only Prince cast out—

Elder, Today, a session wiser
And fainter, too, as Wiseness is—
I find myself still softly searching
For my Delinquent Palaces—

Emily Dickinson

Compared with Ahab's grim vision, Ishmael's vision in "The Whiteness of the Whale" might seem to offer the reader of *Moby-Dick* only a choice between the frying pan and the fire. One might even come to prefer Ahab's sense of cosmic evil (his demonically inverted Transcendentalism) to Ishmael's intuition of an annihilating cosmic emptiness ("the colorless, all-color of atheism") on the Faulknerian grounds that between grief and nothing one should take grief. On the other hand, one might reflect that a blank whiteness is not the only color in the Ishmaelean spectrum and that in aggregate Ahab's univocal, unswerving vision is less desirable than Ishmael's more equivocal and varied view. Before choosing the latter's, however, the reflective reader will first want to consider carefully how much weight can ultimately be given to the items that make up Ishmael's more positive side, and ask how seriously one can take his intuitions of harmony, felicity, and interdependence.

Let us consider the most important items at the colorful end of his spectrum. One of them is the description of the *all* feeling experienced by a lookout standing "a hundred feet above the silent decks" in "The Mast-Head" (chap. 35). When this passage was examined in an earlier chapter, no mention was made of the crucial admonition with which it concludes. "But while this sleep, this dream is on ye," cautions Ishmael, "move your hand or foot an inch; slip your hold at all; and your identity," which has become merged with that of the mystic ocean, "comes back in horror." And even at midday in the fairest weather, you may "drop through that transparent air into the summer sea, no more to rise for ever." The implication is clear: a transporting sense of oneness with the visible world causes a temporary loss of the sense of individual identity— a contingent and vulnerable condition that has as its bottom line not a transient sense of immortality but the abiding awareness of mortality.

A second important item is found in "A Bower in the Arsacides" (chap. 102), in which Ishmael the narrator describes how he once visited "my late royal friend Tranquo, king of Tranque, one of the Arsacides," who took him to see the skeleton of a giant sperm whale that had been carefully transported from the shore to a verdant inland glen. "It was a wondrous sight," says Ishmael, who goes on to describe how the earth beneath was "as a weaver's loom, with a gorgeous carpet on it, whereof the ground-vine tendrils formed the warp and woof, and the living flowers the figures." All the surrounding trees with their laden branches, all the shrubs, ferns and grasses, and the "message-carrying air" are unceasingly active, while through the leaves the sun seems "a flying shuttle weaving the unwearied verdure." Amid this "green, life-restless loom" the great white skeleton of the whale, himself all woven over with vines, seems a weaver-god as every month he assumes "greener, fresher verdure; but himself a skeleton. Life folded Death: Death trellised Life; the grim god wived with youthful Life, and begat him curly-headed glories."

What is suggested by this extraordinary image is, of course, a fusion or synthesis of the dominant land-sea contrast in *Moby-Dick*. If one is reminded of the symbolic reverie of Ishmael the character in "The Mat-Maker" (chap. 47), the comparison only serves to sharpen one's sense of the greater complexity and suggestiveness of the Arsacidian Loom of Time. It includes the whale within it, whereas Ishmael's reverie in "The Mat-Maker" was, we remember, abruptly terminated by the cry of "There she blows!" When one thinks about how seriously the image can be taken, however, certain difficulties arise. For one thing, there is the disconcerting suggestion in the text that the scene resembles a textile factory. More disturbing is the context in which the image is situated. Tranquo and Tranque are both fictitious; and aside from most of the description of the wondrous sight, the style in which the chapter is narrated is a cross between that of the man-of-the-world raconteur, which always in *Moby-Dick* carries bogus overtones, and the voice of the zany picker-up-of-learning's-crumbs, who at the close of the chapter announces that he will set down the skeleton's dimensions "copied verbatim from my right arm, where I had them tattooed; as in my wild wanderings at the period, there was no other secure way of preserving such valuable statistics."

In "The Bower in the Arsacides," then, the positive implications of a visionary moment are to some extent qualified by its context. In the last passage I want to examine, the visionary moment is more than qualified by both its context and the way in which it is presented; it is so undercut as to become a carnivalization of its subject. I refer to the well-known squeezing-the-sperm episode in chapter 94 ("A Squeeze of the Hand"), in which Ishmael the narrator describes how his younger self and some other crewmen once spent the morning "in a sweet and unctuous duty": squeezing back into fluid the lumps that had formed in a large vat of whale sperm. As the *Pequod* glides serenely along under a blue, tranquil sky, Ishmael bathes his hands among "those soft, gentle globules of infiltrated tissues, woven almost within the hour," which discharge their opulence "like fully ripe grapes their wine," and exude "an uncontaminated aroma . . . like the smell of spring violets." Employing a third land-based image, Ishmael declares that "for a time I lived as in a musky meadow; I forgot all about our horrible oath. . . . I felt divinely free from all ill-will, or petulance, or malice, of any sort whatsoever." What Ishmael is beginning to experience is a version of the *all* feeling, a moment of expanded consciousness in which boundaries and divisions seem dissolved in a transporting

sense of unity. What is distinctive about this particular visionary
moment is that it is less cosmic than fraternal, less concerned with
Platonic essences than with the celebration of ordinary ecstasies,
of what Emerson called the pot luck of the day:

> Squeeze! squeeze! squeeze! all the morning long; I squeezed
> that sperm till I myself almost melted into it; I squeezed that
> sperm till a strange sort of insanity came over me; and I found
> myself unwittingly squeezing my co-laborers' hands in it, mistak-
> ing their hands for the gentle globules. Such an abounding, affec-
> tionate, friendly, loving feeling did this avocation beget; that at
> last I was continually squeezing their hands, and looking up into
> their eyes sentimentally; as much as to say,—Oh! my dear fellow
> beings, why should we longer cherish any social acerbities, or
> know the slightest ill-humor or envy! Come; let us squeeze hands
> all round; nay, let us all squeeze ourselves into each other; let us
> squeeze ourselves universally into the very milk and sperm of
> kindness.
>
> Would that I could keep squeezing that sperm for ever! For
> now, since by many prolonged, repeated experiences, I have per-
> ceived that in all cases man must eventually lower, or at least
> shift, his conceit of attainable felicity; not placing it anywhere in
> the intellect or the fancy; but in the wife, the heart, the bed, the
> table, the saddle, the fire-side, the country; now that I have per-
> ceived all this, I am ready to squeeze case eternally. In thoughts
> of the visions of the night, I saw long rows of angels in paradise,
> each with his hands in a jar of spermaceti.

It is important to note that this passage is not the conclusion of
"A Squeeze of the Hand." The chapter ends with the description
of a different activity on a whaling ship, one that balances and
implicitly qualifies the positive implications of the sperm squeezing. This concluding scene takes place below decks in the blubber
room where the large blanket pieces stripped and hoisted from the
whale are cut up. "This apartment is a scene of terror to all tyros,"
says the narrator, especially at night when by the light of a dull
lantern one glimpses pairs of workmen with hooks and specially
sharp spades working on a slippery surface. The result is not a

chummy squeezing of hands but a severing of toes, which "are scarce among veteran blubber-room men."

More importantly, the "squeeze, squeeze, squeeze" passage is undercut from within. There are first of all the patent overtones of what one commentator calls a "homosexual pastoral" and another a celebration of "communal masturbation."[82] That the scene is described in so excessively gushy and sentimental a way also suggests that it is not meant to be read straight, but as a deliberate trivialization of its subject. Any doubts on this score are dispelled when one reaches the bizarre "vision of the night" with which the passage concludes. The long rows of angels in paradise, each with his hands in a jar of spermaceti, is the parodic apotheosis of the squeezing of the sperm, as the celestial ejaculations of the seraphim mirror in a finer tone the masturbatory and exhibitionistic excesses of the description of the sailors at the sperm vat.

It is true that the gushy tone of the passage changes briefly near the beginning of the second quoted paragraph, when Ishmael stands back from the sperm vat to generalize about the need for man to "lower, or at least shift, his conceit of attainable felicity." The note struck here is one often heard in the literature of the nineteenth century and it might be thought unaffected by its context. A number of the central texts of the period carry the message that the only positive alternatives to fruitless introspection, brooding self-conciousness, and unrealizable fantasies are felicities attainable by all human beings but more easily secured by ordinary, unself-conscious persons whose intellectual and imaginative faculties have not been disproportionately developed by the philosophical and religious uncertainties of the time. But neither Ishmael the narrator nor his creator is a George Eliot or a Tolstoy. The common denominator of the wife, the bed, the table, the saddle, the fireside, the country is that they are all land-based and exclusively associated with the values of the shore—with all that's kind to our mortalities and with the insular Tahiti. What is missing from the squeezing-the-sperm vision is any awareness or acknowledgment of the world of the sea. Just as the sperm vat is complemented by the blubber room in chapter 94, so attainable felicities must be balanced by a recognition of ungraspable phantoms. Not to do so

inevitably contaminates through sentimentality any vision of felicity, a process that the sperm-squeezing episode enacts.

There would be no need to underline this point if so much were
not at stake. A major interpretative perspective on *Moby-Dick*
holds that the positive message of the book, the alternative to
Ahab's destructive fatalism and the nihilistic vision that sometimes
overwhelms Ishmael, is love or fellow-feeling. In the sperm-squeezing scene, says Sherman Paul, Ishmael experiences "the redemptive
force of brotherhood" and is saved at the end because "he learns
[the] lesson of human solidarity."[83] Newton Arvin, another excellent critic, agrees: the positive alternative to both Ahab's egotism
and Starbuck's Christian submissiveness is, he says, an "essentially
humanistic and secular principle" which takes the form of "a
strong intuition of human solidarity as a priceless good."[84] But if
the sperm-squeezing scene cannot be cited in support of this con-
tention, what evidence can be brought forward? The bedroom ca-
maraderie of Ishmael and Queequeg at the Spouter-Inn, where the
homoerotic pastoral motif first appears? Surely not, for these
scenes invite the same kind of critical analysis as does the sperm-
squeezing scene. The reflections of Ishmael in "The Monkey-Rope"
(chap. 72) in which he feels "my own individuality . . . now merged
in a joint stock company of two"? Again the answer is no; these
pat ruminations must be assigned to Ishmael the character, not to
his older narratorial self, whose ideal crew member is not Queequeg but the apotheosized Bulkington—the man who struggles to
stay clear of the treacherous, slavish shore on which wives, saddles,
firesides, and so on are found. The fact of the matter is that attempts to find a redemptive force of brotherhood in *Moby-Dick*
are wistful, and can no more withstand close examination than can
Ishmael's own sonorities in "A Squeeze of the Hand."

If a "way to the Better there be," says Thomas Hardy in "In
Tenebris," "it exacts a full look at the Worst." To read *Moby-Dick*
aright, such a full look entails at least two unflinching observations: that Ishmael's positive reflections and even his purposive assertions are usually qualified in a negative way; and that there are
profound affinities between Ishmael's vision and Ahab's, the deepest need of both being not human solidarity but psychic wholeness.

Only after these observations have been fully registered is one in a position to see distinctly how Ishmael's vision may differ from Ahab's.

Let us first recall two key Ishmaelean pronouncements and place them in their immediate contexts. The first is the quintessentially important notion of "the ungraspable phantom of life." In "Loomings" the phrase is used in connection not only with the weekend meditators who are drawn to the land's edge, but also with "the meaning of that story of Narcissus, who because he could not grasp the tormenting, mild image he saw in the fountain, plunged into it and was drowned." That is to say, the phantom of life is for Ishmael not ungraspable in the upbeat, Browningesque sense of reach necessarily exceeding grasp or what's a heaven for. The implication is rather that the pursuit of that self-mirroring ideal can be as destructive on the speculative level as the *Pequod*'s pursuit of the white whale is on the narrative level—a connection nicely suggested by Ishmael himself at the end of chapter 52 when he speaks of "that demon phantom that, sometime or other, swims before all human hearts; while chasing such over this round globe, they either lead us on in barren mazes or midway leave us whelmed." Another Ishmaelean postulate crucially modified by its context is found at the end of chapter 76: "For unless you own the whale, you are but a provincial and sentimentalist in Truth. But clear Truth is a thing for salamander giants only to encounter: how small the chances for the provincials then? What befel the weakling youth lifting the dread goddess's veil at Sais?" What happened to this youth was that he was stricken senseless and died prematurely. What happens to humans who lack the salamander's fabled ability to live in fire is that they get burned up—or, at the speculative level, burned out. The difference, then, between owning and not owning the whale would seem to be between sentimental stagnation in the provinces or incineration on the borders of the unknown—what in "The Lee Shore" is called perishing in the howling infinite.

Against this background, the similarities between Ishmael and Ahab stand out. Both own the whale and both turn their backs on the assuagements and certainties of the land to encounter the perils of the unknown, even though it seems in the cards that, like Pip, they will not survive the experience with all their faculties intact, if they survive at all. Perhaps the most fundamental affinity between the two, however, is found not out there on the borders of the howling infinite but down there in their shared sense of what Ishmael, in referring to Ahab, calls "the subterranean miner that works in us all" (chap. 41). Another striking image of this something deep within is found at the end of the great speech in "The Gilder" (chap. 114):

> Oh, grassy glades! Oh, ever vernal endless landscapes in the soul; in ye,—though long parched by the dead drought of the earthy life,—in ye, men yet may roll, like young horses in new morning clover; and for some few fleeting moments, feel the cool dew of the life immortal on them. Would to God these blessed calms would last. But the mingled, mingling threads of life are woven by warp and woof: calms crossed by storms, a storm for every calm. There is no steady unretracing progress in this life; we do not advance through fixed gradations, and at the last one pause:—through infancy's unconscious spell, boyhood's thoughtless faith, adolescence' doubt (the common doom), then scepticism, then disbelief, resting at last in manhood's pondering repose of If. But once gone through, we trace the round again; and are infants, boys, and men and Ifs eternally. Where lies the final harbor, whence we unmoor no more? In what rapt ether sails the world, of which the weariest will never weary? Where is the foundling's father hidden? Our souls are like those orphans whose unwedded mothers die in bearing them: the secret of our paternity lies in their grave, and we must there to learn it.

Some commentators on this passage are troubled by the question of to whom it should be assigned. The editors of more than one edition of *Moby-Dick*, for example, have emended the passage by placing it in quotation marks, thus assigning it to Ahab, who is the subject of the preceding paragraph. Clearly, these scholars have taken such a drastic editorial step because they thought that otherwise the paragraph might be taken to be Ishmael's rather than Ahab's. If the text of "The Gilder" is looked at carefully, however, it is hard to see why any emendation was thought necessary. There are places elsewhere in *Moby-Dick* where Ishmael the narrator is unquestionably reporting the thoughts or speech of Ahab even though the passage is not placed in quotation marks; and in "The Gilder" it seems clear beyond reasonable doubt that the quoted paragraph presents Ahab's response to a particularly beautiful day, just as an earlier paragraph gives Ishmael's response and subsequent paragraphs those of Starbuck and Stubb.

Taken out of context, however, it is not hard to see how the speech in "The Gilder" could be thought Ishmael's as easily as Ahab's. The images of the foundling's father, the orphanlike soul, and the secret of our paternity, for example, have important reverberations with both characters. In an earlier chapter, we noted that Ahab was an orphan and discussed, inter alia, the Hotel de Cluny image, which speaks of a grim sire buried far below the surface, from whose stony lips alone can "the old State-secret" be revealed to the "young exiled royalties." And when in "The Symphony" (chap. 132) it is said of Ahab that "the step-mother world, so long cruel—forbidding—now threw affectionate arms round his stubborn neck," one thinks at once of Ishmael, who had a cruel stepmother and who in the last words of *Moby-Dick* is referred to as "another orphan." The images of exiled royalty, spiritual orphans, and ancestral secrets that hold the key to an individual's existence all suggest that Ahab and Ishmael both suffer from some primal sense of loss and have a consequent longing for the true life known only through its absence. It is the same spiritual condition so movingly outlined in the poem of Melville's younger contemporary, Emily Dickinson, which is quoted at the beginning of this chapter. Dickinson speaks of an abiding sense of spiritual dispossession, the feeling that there exists somewhere a kingdom that is her birthright but of which she has never come into possession, even while never ceasing to be haunted by a sense of deprivation. The speech in "The Gilder" ends with the assertion that this wound of deprivation can never be repaired in this life, that the "final harbor" can never be reached. There can be no steady progress in life, only a repetitive cycle that must be retraced over and over, only infrequently assuaged by "blessed calms," which are described (as one has come to expect in *Moby-Dick*) in land-based images—vernal landscapes, young horses in new morning clover, the cool dew. For both Ahab and Ishmael, the blessed calms are not illusory; but they are transient. What abides is the awareness that in the loom of human life there is at least one storm for every calm and that this repetition can only be broken by the final harbor of the grave.

One's final answer, then, to the question of whether the great speech in "The Gilder" is Ishmael's or Ahab's is that it does not really matter because at the level probed by the speech there is no essential difference in kind between them. This does not mean, however, that there is no significant difference in degree. For one thing, if we say that Ishmael is a self-conscious narrator who projects onto Ahab his own deepest speculations and psychological anxieties, it would seem ipso facto to follow that Ishmael's vision is more comprehensive than Ahab's and to some extent contains it. For another, there is one chapter in *Moby-Dick* in which Ishmael's reflections are at their most considered and comprehensive and in which he draws a clear distinction in degree between his vision of the world and Ahab's. Ishmael's vision is of course much too open-ended and problematic for any one series of his reflections to be called definitive. But in "The Try-Works" (chap. 96) he offers the most inclusive and conclusive assessment of his own spiritual condition vis-à-vis Ahab's to be found in *Moby-Dick*.

"The Try-Works" begins with a description of the apparatus on the deck of the *Pequod*—two large pots, each of several barrels capacity, placed on top of two furnaces fitted with heavy iron doors—used to boil down the blubber of the sperm whale. It is nine o'clock at night when the tryworks are first started "on this present voyage"; by midnight they are in full operation. It is a remarkable scene. The smoke from the fires—its fuel is fritters of dried whale blubber—"is horrible to inhale, and inhale it you must, and not only that, but you must live in it for the time." The surrounding darkness of the wild ocean is intensified by the light from the fierce flames of the furnace, "which at intervals forked forth from the sooty flues, and illuminated every lofty rope in the rigging." As the pagan harpooneers stoke the furnace and pitch hissing masses of blubber into the scalding pots, "the rushing Pequod, freighted with savages, and laden with fire, and burning a corpse, and plunging into that blackness of darkness, seemed the material counterpart of her monomaniac commander's soul."

So it seemed to Ishmael the character, as he stood at the helm of the *Pequod* "and for long hours silently guided the way of this fire-ship on the sea." Ishmael the narrator goes on to say that the sight before his younger self "at last begat kindred visions" in his soul, and he began to yield to that "unaccountable drowsiness, which ever would come over [me] at a midnight helm." That is to say, a sense of the spiritual fact—of which the natural fact of the scene is the symbol—begins to absorb all his awareness. "A stark, bewildered feeling, as of death, came over me." Only at the last moment does he realize that during "this unnatural hallucination of the night" he has turned around and is facing the blackness of the sea with his back to the ship's prow and compass. He swings back just in time to grasp the helm and keep the *Pequod* from flying up into the wind, and very probably capsizing. The nightmarish vision preceded by an unaccountable drowsiness is similar in kind but antithetical in content to the heaven-on-earth reveries of the younger Ishmael, for example, the one described in "The Mast-Head." The immediate moral of both is the same, however. Just as the individual finite identity of the gazer at the masthead will come back to him in horror if he moves his hand or foot an inch and loses his precarious hold, so the vision of "The Try-Works" almost leads to the capsizing of the *Pequod*.

In the three closing paragraphs of the chapter, Ishmael the narrator makes a series of reflective comments on the unnatural hallucination he experienced. But his train of thought moves beyond the particular experience to more general considerations that include a comparison of his mature vision of human existence and Ahab's. One must not look "too long in the face of the fire" lest one become inverted and deadened. One must not believe only in "the artificial fire" and forget that tomorrow, in the natural sun—"the glorious golden, glad sun, the only true lamp"—the world will look very different. In other words, to recall "The Gilder" speech, the storm will be followed by a calm. Nevertheless, Ishmael continues, one must recognize that the sun cannot hide the fact that even on land there exists grief-laden symbols like Virginia's Dismal

Swamp, "Rome's accursed Campagna," and the wide Sahara. Nor does the sun hide the ocean "which is the dark side of the earth, and which is two thirds of this earth." Ishmael is not saying what Ahab says at the end of chapter 127 (in a passage clearly meant to be compared with Ishmael's statement): that he is so far gone "in the dark side of the earth, that its other side, the theoretic bright one, seems but uncertain twilight to me." But Ishmael is saying something similar in kind: that "the mortal man who hath more of joy than sorrow in him, that moral man cannot be true—not true, or undeveloped" (as we have seen, a leading example of such a man is Starbuck). This being so, Ishmael continues, the truest of all men is the one described in Isaiah (53:3), "a man of sorrows, and acquainted with grief." And the truest of all books is that of Solomon (the Book of Ecclesiastes), "the fine hammered steel of woe," that does not speak to someone (like an educated Stubb) who "dodges hospitals and jails . . . would rather talk of operas than hell . . . and throughout a carefree lifetime swears by Rabelais as passing wise, and therefore jolly."

In the chapter's final paragraph, Ishmael again urges his reader (and himself) to "Give not thyself up, then, to fire, lest it invert thee, deaden thee; as for the time it did me." The man in *Moby-Dick* who does give himself up completely to fire (vide "The Candles") is Ahab, and it is to him as well as to himself that Ishmael refers in his next sentence: "There is a wisdom that is woe; but there is a woe that is madness." Here is encapsulated the crucial difference in degree between the two dominant figures in the work. The older Ishmael, a man of sorrows and acquainted with grief, has, or aspires to, a wisdom that is woe, that recognizes that just as the oceans cover most of the earth, so sorrow and not joy is predominant in human experience. Ahab recognizes this too, but his exasperations have moved him one crucial degree closer to the fire than Ishmael; the woe of Ahab has become a madness in which joy or sunlight is merely theoretical and can be no longer felt (as he had recognized in his early soliloquy in the significantly titled "Sunset" chapter).

Having made this crucial distinction, however, Ishmael ends his meditation with a superlative natural image that reaffirms both his and Ahab's essential similarity and the grandeur that their tragic recognitions give them. There is, he says, "a Catskill eagle in some souls that can alike dive down into the blackest gorges, and soar out of them again and become invisible in the sunny spaces." Even if this eagle "for ever flies within the gorge, that gorge is in the mountains," so that in its lowest swoop it is still higher than the birds of the plain even when they soar—higher, that is, than the Queequegs, the Flasks, the Stubbs, the Starbucks, and all those who cannot or will not explore the blackness within them.

X: The Ending

The Mariner, whose eye is bright,
Whose beard with age is hoar,
Is gone: and now the Wedding-Guest
Turned from the bridegroom's door.

He went like one that hath been stunned,
And is of sense forlorn:
A sadder and a wiser man,
He rose the morrow morn.

Coleridge, "The Rime of the Ancient Mariner"

The last three chapters of *Moby-Dick*, which describe the *Pequod*'s three-day battle with the great white whale, make a spectacular conclusion to a narrative that for most of its length has been episodic and digressive. But as a recent commentator has remarked, while the book "is magnificently resolved at the level of action, [it is] magnificently unresolved at the level of meaning."[85] One might even say that on the latter level the ending reflects an insight into life and into fiction similar to that of the would-be novelist and title character of *Pierre*, the novel that Melville began writing as soon as *Moby-Dick* was behind him:

By infallible presentiment [Pierre] saw, that not always doth life's beginning gloom conclude in gladness; that wedding-bells peal not ever in the last scene of life's fifth act; that while the countless tribes of common novels laboriously spin veils of mystery, only to complacently clear them up at last; and while the countless tribe of common dramas do but repeat the same; yet the profounder emanations of the human mind, intended to illustrate all that can be humanly known of human life; these never unravel their own intricacies, and have no proper endings; but in imperfect, unanticipated, and disappointing sequels (as mutilated stumps), hurry to abrupt intermergings with the eternal tides of time and fate.[86]

The reference to mutilated stumps might even tempt one to think that earlier in *Moby-Dick* Ishmael had sketched a picture of himself as artist in the description of the crippled beggar on the London docks that opens chapter 57. This man of sorrow says nothing, but simply holds before him a painted board representing the tragic scene in which he lost his leg while, "with downcast eyes, [he] stands ruefully contemplating his own amputation."

On the other hand, there are two salient features of the closing pages of *Moby-Dick* that not only invite interpretative commentary but also seem, if not to offer an unraveling of the work's intricacies, at least to supply opportunities to reflect on what has gone before. They allow one to place the book in a perhaps more disinterested and distanced (I do not say authorial or authoritative) perspective than that supplied by Ishmael the narrator. One of these features is the white whale itself, which in the closing pages of *Moby-Dick* finally appears in propria persona. One might reasonably ask if there is any implicit meaning in the presented natural fact of Moby Dick that either confirms or differs from the meanings projected onto him by Ahab, by Ishmael in "The Whiteness of the Whale," or by others in the book. Can the reader of *Moby-Dick*, whose experience of the text has provided a careful schooling in symbolic perception, find a fresh significance lurking in the white whale?

The reader and the crew of the *Pequod* both see Moby Dick for the first time in chapter 133 when he is observed "heading straight to leeward . . . right away from us." The boat crews give chase and at length

> his entire dazzling hump was distinctly visible, sliding along the sea as if an isolated thing, and continually set in a revolving ring of finest, fleecy, greenish foam. [One] saw the vast, involved wrinkles of the slightly projecting head beyond. Before it, far out on the soft Turkish-rugged waters, went the glistening white shadow from his broad, milky forehead, a musical rippling playfully accompanying the shade; and behind, the blue waters interchangeably flowed over into the moving valley of his steady wake; and on either hand bright bubbles arose and danced by his side. But these were broken again by the light toes of

hundreds of gay fowl softly feathering the sea, alternate with
their fitful flight; and like to some flag-staff rising from the painted hull of an argosy, the tall but shattered pole of a recent lance
projected from the white whale's back; and at intervals one of
the cloud of soft-toed fowls hovering, and to and fro skimming
like a canopy over the fish, silently perched and rocked on this
pole, the long tail feathers streaming like pennons.

A gentle joyousness—a mighty mildness of repose in swiftness,
invested the gliding whale . . . as he so divinely swam.

This description places the white whale before the reader not only
in all his living power but also in all his sublime attractiveness: the
hump dazzles, bright bubbles dance, a musical rippling plays
around his bulk, and gay fowls feather the sea, while greenish
foam, a glistening whiteness, and blue water add color to the scene.
Any suspicion that the description is perhaps a shade idealized or
unrealistically touched up is put to rest by the vivid authenticating
detail of the silent bird perched and rocking on the top of the shattered pole sticking from the whale's back. A few paragraphs later
it is the power and awesomeness of the white whale that are em-
phasized: having sounded, Moby Dick eventually begins to breach,
at first appearing in the depths of the water as "a white living spot
no bigger than a white weasel," then rising "with wonderful celer-
ity" until "this tremendous apparition" is again fully before the
viewer.

It is true that after the initial description of the white whale the
narrator ominously remarks that the alluring serenity and enticing
calm of his ambiance had previously attracted hunters who had
"fatally found that quietude but the vesture of tornadoes." It is also
true that when, after breaching, Moby Dick becomes aware that
he is under attack, he is said to display "that malicious intelligence
ascribed to him." But the fact that the whale does not adopt a
posture of Christian submissiveness towards his pursuers does not
necessarily mean that his intelligence is malicious or that he is the
incarnation of an inscrutable malice or of the heartless voids and
immensities of the universe. And if the wondrous phenomenon of
his breaching and other descriptive touches suggest a profound sex-

ual energy, it does not follow that these phallic overtones serve only to emphasize the whale's destructive power (as one astute commentator thinks they do).[87] For the sexuality of Moby Dick also calls to mind the lovely description of "the nursing mothers of the whales" in "The Grand Armada" (chap. 87), a profoundly sexual scene, the peace of which is interrupted by the hideous sight of the frantic whales who have been cruelly drugged (had their tail-tendons sundered or maimed) by their pursuers. In this scene, as in the scene in which Moby Dick first appears, violence and destructive malice are initiated by the human hunters, not by the sperm whales, who when left to themselves seem magnificently self-sufficient and unaggressive. Nor should one fail to notice that in the chapter describing the final day of the chase, alternative explanations are suggested as to why Moby Dick's pace begins to abate. Ishmael cannot say with certainty whether this is caused by the fatigue of "the three days' running chase, and the resistance to his swimming in the knotted hamper he bore," or is owing to "some latent deceitfulness and malice in him."

I do not mean to say that the great white whale does not possess an awesome destructive potential, but that the text of the closing chapters of *Moby-Dick* suggests that destructiveness is not the white whale's defining characteristic nor his raison d'être. One should rather say of Moby Dick what Shelley says of the similarly awe-inspiring mountain in "Mount Blanc"—"the power is there." Shelley cannot say what the source of this power is, whether an implacable hostility to man is part of its essence, or even whether the power is creative-and-destructive instead of only the latter. But he has absolutely no doubt that this sublime power exists and that "the secret strength of things" inhabits it. In the same way, when Ishmael studied the severed head of a sperm whale in chapter 79, he was forced to conclude that its meaning could never be discovered, for there is "no Champollion to decipher the Egypt of every man's and every being's face." All Ishmael could say to the reader was that "I but put that brow before you. Read it if you can." But he was certain that the aspect of the full front of the whale's head was "sublime," that a "high and mighty god-like dignity" was inherent in it, and that in gazing on it "you feel the Deity and the dread powers more forcibly than in beholding any other object in living nature."

What is true of Shelley's Mont Blanc and the severed head of the sperm whale is equally true of Moby Dick the whale. In an analogous way it is also true of *Moby-Dick* the book. Nina Baym puts the matter very well: "The ultimate impression conveyed by *Moby-Dick* is that the quest for truth is significant and meaningful even if no truth is attained and that a book embodying such a quest is certainly meaningful and significant."[88] The meanings of *Moby-Dick* are, then, considerations secondary to the sustained power of the book in presenting the quest for what its opening chapter called "the ungraspable phantom of life." What *Moby-Dick* magnificently gives the reader is Ishmael's sense of what Melville called "visable truth." At the end of chapter 110 Ishmael describes the "hieroglyphic marks" that "a departed prophet and seer of his island" had tattooed on Queequeg's living body. Though "his own live heart" beat against these mysterious signs, Queequeg could not decipher them and they "were therefore destined in the end to moulder away with the living parchment whereon they were inscribed." The mysteries that Ishmael tries to decipher are less perishable not because he is able to unravel their intricacies but because of the power of his mighty book to leave a lasting impression on the minds and emotions of its readers.

The other opportunity for retrospective reflection provided by the close of *Moby-Dick* is its epilogue. The epilogue did not appear in the first (British) edition of the book and it seems reasonable to think that the primary reason for its composition and inclusion was to explain how the first-person narrator survived to tell the tale. But its two paragraphs do much more than simply satisfy the reader's curiosity:

> The Drama's done. Why then here does any one step forth?—
> Because one did survive the wreck.
>   It so chanced, that after the Parsee's disappearance, I was he whom the Fates ordained to take the place of Ahab's bowsman, when that bowsman assumed the vacant post; the same, who, when on the last day the three men were tossed from out the

rocking boat, was dropped astern. So, floating on the margin of the ensuing scene, and in full sight of it, when the half-spent suction of the sunk ship reached me, I was then, slowly, drawn towards the closing vortex. When I reached it, it had subsided to a creamy pool. Round and round, then, and ever contracting towards the button-like black bubble at the axis of that slowly wheeling circle, like another Ixion I did revolve. Till, gaining that vital centre, the black bubble upward burst; and now, liberated by reason of its cunning spring, and, owing to its great buoyancy, rising with great force, the coffin life-buoy shot lengthwise from the sea, fell over, and floated by my side. Buoyed up by that coffin, for almost one whole day and night, I floated on a soft and dirge-like main. The unharming sharks, they glided by as if with padlocks on their mouths; the savage sea-hawks sailed with sheathed beaks. On the second day, a sail drew near, nearer, and picked me up at last. It was the devious-cruising Rachel, that in her retracing search after her missing children, only found another orphan.

One of the first things the careful reader of *Moby-Dick* will notice about the epilogue is that it presents alternative possibilities. One of them concerns causality. "I was he whom the Fates ordained," says Ishmael, thereby suggesting the same supernatural explanation of the events at the end of the book as Ahab does on the second day of the chase when he tells Starbuck that "the whole act's immutably decreed" and that "I am the Fates' lieutenant; I act under orders" (chap. 134). But Ishmael begins the very sentence in which he mentions fate by saying "It so chanced," thereby raising the possibility not that his survival was preordained but that he simply lucked out at the end. One further notes that Ishmael is careful to supply a matter-of-fact, naturalistic explanation for the enabling condition of his survival: it was "by reason of its cunning spring, and, owing to its great buoyancy," that the coffin life buoy came to shoot from the sea and float next to him.

The allusions to, or echoes of, earlier moments in the book also suggest alternative interpretations. Some of these associations are negative or pessimistic in their implications about the meaning of the epilogue. Ishmael's floating alone on the boundless expanse of midocean only to be picked up by the merest chance recalls the earlier experience of Pip in "The Castaway," as a result of which his finite body survived but the infinite in his soul drowned. And the dreamy unnaturalness of the scene—the unharming sharks with padlocked jaws, the savage sea hawks with sheathed beaks— recalls those daytime ocean reveries of Ishmael the character, which are more than once explicitly criticized in the text. And the last word of the epilogue—*orphan*—inevitably recalls the end of Ahab's speech in "The Gilder" and might therefore be thought to endorse the grim message that the secret of our paternity lies in the grave.

On the other hand, it is equally possible to read the epilogue in a more positive way. For one thing, its tone is hardly that of "The Gilder" speech. It is calm and dirgelike, even elegiac, and conveys a strong sense of all passion spent. And it involves the story of a grieving father searching for his lost son. The father is Captain Gardiner—his very name suggests the values of the land as opposed to the sea—who in chapter 128 had movingly beseeched Ahab to assist in the search for his "missing boy; a little lad, but twelve years old." The name of his ship is the *Rachel,* that archetypal Old Testament figure of parental loss who wept bitterly for her children and "refused to be comforted . . . because they were not" (Jer. 31:15). And one also may be reminded that the late chapter, which describes how Queequeg's coffin came to be turned into a coffin life buoy, has near its beginning the description of the affecting sound of "the young seals that had lost their dams, or some dams that had lost their cubs . . . crying and sobbing with their human sort of wail" (chap. 126). In the epilogue, then, human pathos supersedes psychological tragedy as the motif of the grieving father searching for his lost son replaces that of the traumatic quest of the orphaned son for the unrecoverable paternal secret. Similarly, the land-sea opposition that is the predominant thematic motif in *Moby-Dick* seems transcended in the epilogue. The savage sharks do not affright; the whiteness of the water does not suggest the demonism of the world and the heartless voids of the universe, but is rather a creamy pool (a land-based image) in the center of which floats a coffin life buoy, which suggests a reconciliation of life and

<u>death and perhaps even intimates that</u> (to borrow a phrase of Philip Larkin's) what will survive of us is love.

And yet, and yet . . . While it is both possible and very tempting to read the epilogue in this way one would not feel at all comfortable about ending a reading of *Moby-Dick* on this note. It is better to remind oneself that Ishmael is both the character who survives the destruction of the *Pequod* and the retrospective narrator who tells the story and whose attempts to find meaning and significance in his material are necessarily tentative and suggestive, never definitive. One might even conclude one's reflections on *Moby-Dick* by asking what happened to Ishmael after the action of the book ended. Such a question might, prima facie, be considered an indication of a naive confusion of life and art. But of a work like *Moby-Dick*, which employs a first-person retrospective narrator, the question can legitimately be asked. The only part of the answer that one knows is that after his adventures on the *Pequod* Ishmael eventually went on to write *Moby-Dick*, which has in it a great deal more sorrow than joy, and which is not an attempt to promulgate any particular truth that Ishmael had learned but to discover the meaning of the events of which he had been a part and to convey to his audience his sense of the profound issues that he feels to be at stake.

One might add that Ishmael's passage from sailor to author is an arc on the circumference of the same repetitive circle that Ahab describes in his speech in "The Gilder." This might in turn suggest that Ishmael the narrator resembles Coleridge's Ancient Mariner (Ishmael admired Coleridge's "wild Rhyme" and spoke of its "noble merit" in chapter 42). At times during his tale the Mariner speaks piously about loving all things both great and small; but his profoundest and most memorable utterances have to do with the spiritual terrors of midocean ("Alone, alone, all, all alone / Alone on a wide wide sea") and he is compelled to repeat his story—to retrace the same round—over and over again. But the figure whom Ishmael the narrator most clearly resembles is not Coleridge's Ancient Mariner but Herman Melville as described by Hawthorne in 1856, five years after publication of *Moby-Dick*. Hawthorne was at the time living in Liverpool as the American consul and it was there that he was visited by Melville, who was on his way to the Holy Land. Here is Hawthorne's memorable picture of the man who when he finished *Moby-Dick* must have known that he had written a mighty book but who only three days after its American publication could say that "as long as we have anything more to do, we have done nothing."[89]

> He stayed with us from Tuesday till Thursday; and, on the intervening day, we took a pretty long walk together, and sat down in a hollow among the sand hills (sheltering ourselves from the high, cool wind) and smoked a cigar. Melville, as he always does, began to reason of Providence and futurity, and of everything that lies beyond human ken, and informed me that he had "pretty much made up his mind to be annihilated"; but still he does not seem to rest in that anticipation; and, I think, will never rest until he gets hold of a definite belief. It is strange how he persists—and has persisted ever since I knew him, and probably long before—in wandering to-and-fro over these deserts, as dismal and monotonous as the sand hills amid which we were sitting. He can neither believe, nor be comfortable in his unbelief; and he is too honest and courageous not to try to do one or the other. If he were a religious man, he would be one of the most truly religious and reverential; he has a very high and noble nature, and better worth immortality than most of us.[90]

Notes and References

1. Herman Melville, "Hawthorne and His Mosses," in *The Portable Melville*, ed. Jay Leyda (New York: Viking, 1952), 409, 410, 411.

2. Larzer Ziff, "Shakespeare and Melville's America," in *New Perspectives on Melville*, ed. Faith Pullin (Edinburgh: Edinburgh University Press, 1978), 57.

3. Ralph Waldo Emerson, *Nature*, in *Essays and Lectures* (New York: Library of America, 1983), 7.

4. Margaret Fuller, "American Literature," in *The Writings of Margaret Fuller*, ed. Mason Wade (New York: Viking, 1941), 358.

5. Walt Whitman, *Song of Myself*, in *Complete Poetry and Selected Prose* (New York: Library of America, 1982), 28.

6. Henry David Thoreau, *Walden*, ed. Sherman Paul (Boston: Houghton Mifflin, 1960), 62–63, 220. For a brief but suggestive comparison of *Walden* and *Moby-Dick* see Sherman Paul, "Resolution at Walden," *Accent* 13 (1953); reprinted in *Interpretations of American Literature*, ed. Charles Feidelson, Jr. and Paul Brodtkorb, Jr. (New York: Oxford University Press, 1959), 165–66.

7. Also see Melville's 1847 *Literary World* review of J. Ross Browne's *Etchings of a Whaling Cruise;* reprinted in the Norton Critical Edition of *Moby-Dick*, ed. Harrison Hayford and Hershel Parker (New York: Norton, 1967), 529.

8. Leo Marx, *The Machine in the Garden: Technology and the Pastoral Ideal in America* (New York: Oxford University Press, 1964), 285, 306.

9. See F. O. Matthiessen, *American Renaissance: Art and Expression in the Age of Emerson and Whitman* (New York: Oxford University Press, 1941), 459. Also see Henry Nash Smith, "The Image of Society in *Moby-Dick*," in *"Moby-Dick": Centennial Essays*, ed. Tyrus Hillway and Luther S. Mansfield (Dallas: Southern Methodist University Press, 1953), 59–75.

10. Quoted in John Stafford, *The Literary Criticism of "Young America": A Study in the Relationship of Politics and Literature 1837–1850* (Berkeley: University of California Press, 1952), 5.

11. Ralph Waldo Emerson, "The American Scholar," in *Essays and Lectures*, 68–69.

12. "Introduction," *Democratic Review* 1 (October 1837):14–15. Quoted in John Stafford, "Henry Norman Hudson and the Whig Use of Shakespeare," *PMLA* 66 (1951):659.

13. Walt Whitman, "A Backward Glance O'er Travel'd Roads," in *Complete Poetry and Selected Prose*, 663.

14. Merrell R. Davis and William H. Gilman, eds., *The Letters of Herman Melville* (New Haven: Yale University Press, 1960), 79–80.

15. M. H. Abrams, *Natural Supernaturalism: Tradition and Revolution in Romantic Literature* (New York: Norton, 1971) is an excellent introduction to its subject.

16. Emerson, *Nature*, 20.

17. Ibid., 10.

18. This phrase is the title of the crucial eighth chapter of the third book of *Sartor Resartus*.

19. Emerson, *Nature*, 7.

20. Thoreau, *Walden*, 214, 216.

21. See Northrop Frye, *A Study of English Romanticism* (New York: Random House, 1968), 15–35.

22. Abrams, *Natural Supernaturalism*, 13.

23. Melville, *Letters*, 130–31.

24. Melville, "Hawthorne and His Mosses," 406–7.

25. Melville, *Letters*, 142.

26. See Millicent Bell, "Pierre Bayle and *Moby-Dick*," *PMLA* 66 (1951): 626–48.

27. Melville, "Hawthorne and His Mosses," 407.

28. Melville, *Letters*, 79.

29. Melville, "Hawthorne and His Mosses," 407.

30. D. H. Lawrence, *Studies in Classic American Literature* (Garden City, New York: Doubleday, 1951), 158. I am misrepresenting a little the context of Lawrence's encomium. He is contrasting Melville's "sheer apprehension of the world" with his "sententious," "self-conscious" and "*grand sérieux*" qualities (157).

31. See my *"Middlemarch"* (London and Boston: Allen & Unwin, 1984), 32–39.

32. David Garnett, ed., *The Letters of T. E. Lawrence* (London: Jonathan Cape, 1938), 360, 548.

33. For an excellent discussion of the tradition of the self-conscious

novel see Robert Alter, *Partial Magic: The Novel as a Self-Conscious Genre* (Berkeley: University of California Press, 1975). Alter defines "a fully self-conscious novel" as "one in which from beginning to end, through the style, the handling of narrative viewpoint, the names and words imposed on the characters, the patterning of the narration, the nature of the characters and what befalls them, there is a consistent effort to convey to us a sense of the fictional world as an authorial construct set up against a background of literary tradition and convention" (xi).

34. George Steiner, *Tolstoy or Dostoevsky: An Essay in the Old Criticism* (New York: Random House, 1961), 13.

35. The idiom is that of reader-response criticism. See especially Wolfgang Iser, "Indeterminacy and the Reader's Response in Prose Fiction," in *Aspects of Narrative: Selected Papers from the English Institute,* ed. J. Hillis Miller (New York: Columbia University Press, 1971), 1–45.

36. Robert Lowell, "Epics," *New York Review of Books,* 21 February 1980, p. 5.

37. Melville, *Letters,* 124, 127, 134, 129, 128.

38. Herman Melville, *Typee, Omoo, Mardi* (New York: Library of America, 1982), 10, 1326, 326.

39. Melville, *Letters,* 70.

40. Ibid., 91–92.

41. Ibid., 109.

42. Melville, "Hawthorne and His Mosses," 410, 413.

43. Robert Midler, "The Composition of *Moby-Dick:* A Review and a Prospect," *Emerson Society Quarterly* 23 (1977):203–16. Midler's discussion builds on and qualifies two other important analyses of the novel's composition: George R. Stewart, "The Two *Moby-Dicks,*" *American Literature* 25 (1954):417–48; and James Barbour, "The Composition of *Moby-Dick,*" *American Literature* 47 (1975):343–60. I am particularly indebted to Barbour and Midler.

44. Harrison Hayford, "Melville and Hawthorne: A Biographical and Critical Study," (Ph.D. diss.: Yale University, 1945), 179; quoted in Midler, 211.

45. Melville, "Hawthorne and His Mosses," 417.

46. Hugh W. Hetherington, "Early Reviews of *Moby-Dick,*" in *Centennial Essays,* ed. Hillway and Mansfield, 119.

47. Quoted in Hetherington, "Early Reviews," 97.

48. Quoted in Watson G. Branch, ed., *Melville: The Critical Heritage* (London and Boston: Routledge & Kegan Paul, 1974), 27. Branch

reprints a generous selection of reviews of *Moby-Dick*. So do Hershel Parker and Harrison Hayford in their *"Moby-Dick" as Doubloon: Essays and Extracts (1851–1970)* (New York: Norton, 1970). Also see Brian Higgins, ed., *Herman Melville: An Annotated Bibliography, vol. 1, 1846–1930* (Boston: G.K. Hall, 1979).

49. William Charvat, "Melville and the Common Reader," *Studies in Bibliography* 12 (1959):41.

50. Melville, *Letters,* 138.

51. Van Wyck Brooks, "A Reviewer's Notebook," in *"Moby-Dick" as Doubloon,* ed. Parker and Hayford, 145, 154.

52. Lewis Mumford, *Herman Melville* (New York: Harcourt Brace, 1929), 181, 182, 184.

53. Leon Howard, *Herman Melville: A Biography* (Berkeley: University of California Press, 1951), 163.

54. Newton Arvin, *Herman Melville* (New York: Sloan, 1950), 169, 170, 181, 183.

55. Henry A. Murray, "In Nomine Diaboli," in *Centennial Essays,* ed. Hillway and Mansfield, 12, 15.

56. Walter E. Bezanson, *"Moby-Dick:* Work of Art," in *Centennial Essays,* ed. Hillway and Mansfield, 36, 41, 45, 46.

57. Charles Feidelson, Jr., *Symbolism and American Literature* (Chicago: University of Chicago Press, 1953), 4, 31, 32.

58. Leslie Fiedler, *Love and Death in the American Novel,* rev. ed. (New York: Stein & Day, 1966), 8, 11, 12, 370.

59. Harry Levin, *The Power of Blackness: Hawthorne, Poe, Melville* (New York: Knopf, 1960), vi.

60. Marius Bewley, *The Eccentric Design: Form in the Classic American Novel* (London: Chatto & Windus, 1959), 192.

61. Franz Stanzel, *Narrative Situations in the Novel: "Tom Jones," "Moby-Dick," "The Ambassadors," "Ulysses",* trans. James P. Pusack (Bloomington: Indiana University Press, 1971), 70–91. Also see Glauco Cambon, "Ishmael and the Problem of Formal Discontinuities in *Moby-Dick," Modern Language Notes* 76 (1961):516–23.

62. Emerson, *Nature,* 10; Wordsworth, *Prelude* (1850), bk. 2, lines 348–52.

63. Thoreau, *Walden,* 221.

64. Heinz Kosok, "Ishmael's Audience in 'The Town-Ho's Story'," *Notes and Queries* 14 (1967):54–56; reprinted in *"Moby-Dick" as Doubloon,* ed. Parker and Hayford, 358–63.

65. See Bezanson, *"Moby-Dick:* Work of Art," 52.

66. Thomas Carlyle, *On Heroes, Hero-Worship, and the Heroic in History,* ed. Archibald MacMechan (Boston: Ginn, 1901), 7.

67. Nina Baym, "Melville's Quarrel with Fiction," *PMLA* 94 (1979):918.

68. Lawrence, *Studies in Classic American Literature,* 172.

69. Paul Merchant, *The Epic* (London: Methuen, 1971), 75.

70. W. P. Ker, *Epic and Romance: Essays on Medieval Literature* (London: Macmillan, 1908), 7–9.

71. See the first chapter of Thomas A. Vogler, *Preludes to Vision: The Epic Venture in Blake, Wordsworth, Keats, and Hart Crane* (Berkeley: University of California Press, 1971).

72. John Stuart Mill, *Literary Essays,* ed. Edward Alexander (Indianapolis: Bobbs-Merrill, 1967), 132.

73. Dwight Culler, *The Poetry of Tennyson* (New Haven: Yale University Press, 1977), 225.

74. See Matthiessen, *American Renaissance,* 426.

75. Samuel Taylor Coleridge, *Notes and Lectures upon Shakespeare,* ed. Mrs. H. N. Coleridge (New York: Harper, 1853), 145.

76. Herman Melville, *The Confidence-Man: His Masquerade,* ed. Elizabeth S. Foster (New York: Hendricks House, 1954), 270–71.

77. Quoted in Henry Nash Smith, "The Madness of Ahab," *Yale Review* 66 (1976):17.

78. Melville, *The Confidence-Man,* 271.

79. Melville, *Typee, Omoo, Mardi,* 235–36, 238, 240.

80. W. H. Auden, "The Christian Tragic Hero," *New York Times Book Review,* 16 December 1945, pp. 1, 21.

81. Matthew Arnold, *The Letters of Matthew Arnold to Arthur Hugh Clough,* ed. Howard Foster Lowry (Oxford: Clarendon Press, 1932), 111.

82. Harold Beaver, ed., *Moby-Dick* (Harmondsworth, England: Penguin Books, 1972), 876; T. Walter Herbert, Jr., "Homosexuality and Spiritual Aspiration in *Moby-Dick,*" *Canadian Review of American Studies* 6 (1975):56.

83. Sherman Paul, Introduction to the Everyman Library edition of *Moby-Dick* (London: Dent, 1961), xi.

84. Arvin, *Herman Melville,* 181.

85. Richard Brodhead, *Hawthorne, Melville, and the Novel* (Chicago: University of Chicago Press, 1976), 161.

86. Herman Melville, *Pierre or, The Ambiguities,* ed. Henry A. Murray (New York: Hendricks House, 1962), 166.

87. See Robert Shulman, "The Serious Function of Melville's Phallic Jokes," *American Literature* 33 (1961):190–94.

88. Baym, "Melville's Quarrel with Fiction," 915.

89. Melville, *Letters,* 143.

90. Nathaniel Hawthorne, *The English Notebooks,* ed. Randall Stewart (New York: Russell & Russell, 1962), 432–33.

Selected Bibliography

Primary Sources

Editions of *Moby-Dick*

Arion Press edition. Berkeley and London: University of California Press, 1981. Trade edition of the 1979 Arion Press edition designed by Andrew Hoyem, with splendid boxwood engravings by Barry Moser illustrating places, creatures, tools, and processess connected with nineteenth-century whaling.

Beaver, Harold, ed. Harmondsworth, England: Penguin, 1972. Includes 279 pages of frequently indiscriminate and sometimes egregious commentary.

Feidelson, Charles, Jr., ed. Indianapolis: Bobbs-Merrill, 1964. Notable for its interpretative commentary on images and symbols.

Hayford, Harrison and Hershel Parker, eds. New York: Norton, 1967. Norton Critical Edition. Includes "Hawthorne and His Mosses," pertinent Melville letters, some contemporary reviews, and a selection of modern criticism.

Hayford, Harrison; Hershel Parker, and G. Thomas Tanselle, eds. Evanston and Chicago: Northwestern University Press and the Newberry Library, forthcoming. Will become the textually authoritative edition of *Moby-Dick*.

Mansfield, Luther S. and Howard P. Vincent, eds. New York: Hendricks House, 1952. Landmark scholarly edition with 264 pages of explanatory notes.

Secondary Sources

Books

ADAMS, ROBERT MARTIN. *Nil: Episodes in the Literary Conquest of the Void During the Nineteenth Century.* New York: Oxford University Press, 1966. Includes discussion of Ishmael as narrator.

ARVIN, NEWTON. *Herman Melville.* American Men of Letters series. New York: Sloane, 1950. Biographical-critical study, with an excellent chapter on *Moby-Dick.*

AUDEN, W. H. *The Enchafèd Flood or The Romantic Iconography of the Sea.* New York: Random House, Vintage Books, 1967.

BAIRD, JAMES. *Ishmael: A Study of the Symbolic Mode in Primitivism.* Baltimore: The Johns Hopkins Press, 1956. Reprint. New York: Harper, 1960.

BERTHOFF, WARNER. *The Example of Melville.* Princeton: Princeton University Press, 1962. Melville "as a writer, a master of expression."

BICKMAN, MARTIN, ed. *Approaches to Teaching Melville's "Moby-Dick."* New York: Modern Language Association of America, 1985.

BRANCH, WATSON G. *Melville: The Critical Heritage.* London: Routledge & Kegan Paul, 1974. Includes twenty-one reviews of *Moby-Dick.*

BRODHEAD, RICHARD H. *Hawthorne, Melville, and the Novel.* Chicago: University of Chicago Press, 1976. Includes excellent chapter on *Moby-Dick.*

BRODTKORB, PAUL, JR. *Ishmael's White World: A Phenomenological Reading of "Moby-Dick."* New Haven: Yale University Press, 1965. Important interpretive monograph.

CHASE, RICHARD. *The American Novel and Its Tradition.* Garden City, New York: Doubleday, Anchor Books, 1957. Reprint. Baltimore: Johns Hopkins University Press, 1980. Romance as the most original and characteristic form of the American novel. Includes a chapter on *Moby-Dick.*

———. *Herman Melville: A Critical Study.* New York: Macmillan, 1949. Stresses folklore in *Moby-Dick.*

COHEN, HENNING and CAHALAN, JAMES, eds. *A Concordance to Melville's "Moby-Dick."* 3 vols. The Melville Society, 1978. Distributed by University Microfilms, Ann Arbor, Mich. Includes alphabetical word index and numerical word index.

DRYDEN, EDGAR A. *Melville's Thematics of Form: The Great Art of Telling the Truth.* Baltimore: Johns Hopkins University Press, 1968. Includes chapter on "Ishmael as Teller: Self-Conscious Form in *Moby-Dick.*"

EDINGER, EDWARD F. *Melville's "Moby-Dick": A Jungian Commentary—An American Nekyia.* New York: New Directions, 1978.

FEIDELSON, CHARLES, JR. *Symbolism and American Literature.* Chicago: University of Chicago Press, 1953.

FIEDLER, LESLIE. *Love and Death in the American Novel.* Rev. ed. New York: Stein & Day, 1966.

FRANKLIN, H. BRUCE. *The Wake of the Gods: Melville's Mythology.* Stanford: Stanford University Press, 1963. Includes chapter on "*Moby-Dick:* An Egyptian Myth Incarnate."

GILMORE, MICHAEL, ed. *Twentieth-Century Interpretations of "Moby-Dick": A Collection of Critical Essays.* Englewood Cliffs, N. J.: Prentice-Hall, 1977. Includes Jean-Paul Sartre's brief comments on *Moby-Dick* as "an enormous summa . . . which [can] only be compared, in its unmeasured hugeness, to Rabelais' *Pantagruel* or James Joyce's *Ulysses.*"

GUETTI, JAMES. *The Limits of Metaphor: A Study of Melville, Conrad, and Faulkner.* Ithaca: Cornell University Press, 1967. Includes chapter on "The Languages of *Moby-Dick.*"

HERBERT, T. WALTER, JR. *"Moby-Dick" and Calvinism: A World Dismantled.* New Brunswick, N. J.: Rutgers University Press, 1977.

HILLWAY, TYRUS. *Herman Melville.* New York: Twayne, 1963. Critical overview, with chapter on *Moby-Dick.*

HILLWAY, TYRUS and MANSFIELD, LUTHER S., eds. *"Moby-Dick": Centennial Essays.* Dallas: Southern Methodist University Press, 1953. Nine essays, including Henry A. Murray's "In Nomine Diaboli" and Walter E. Bezanson's "*Moby-Dick:* Work of Art."

HOFFMAN, DANIEL G. *Form and Fable in American Fiction.* New York: Oxford University Press, 1961. Includes chapter on "Myth, Magic and Metaphor in *Moby-Dick.*"

HOWARD, LEON. *Herman Melville: A Biography.* Berkeley: University of California Press, 1951. The standard life; seventh chapter discusses the genesis of *Moby-Dick.*

KAWIN, BRUCE F. *The Mind of the Novel: Reflexive Fiction and the Ineffable.* Princeton: Princeton University Press, 1982. Discusses *Moby-Dick* in chapter on "Metaphysical Heroism: The Second First Person."

LAWRENCE, D. H. *Studies in Classic American Literature.* Garden City, N. Y.: Doubleday, Anchor Books, 1951. The penultimate chapter of Lawrence's classic study is on *Moby-Dick.*

LEYDA, JAY. *The Melville Log: A Documentary Life of Herman Melville 1819–1891.* 2 vols. New York: Harcourt, Brace, 1951. All the biographical facts.

MARX, LEO. *The Machine in the Garden: Technology and the Pastoral Ideal in America.* New York: Oxford University Press, 1964. Includes substantial interpretative discussion of *Moby-Dick.*

MATTHIESSEN, F. O. *American Renaissance: Art and Expression in the Age of Emerson and Whitman.* New York: Oxford University Press, 1941. Includes substantial discussion of *Moby-Dick.*

MILLER, EDWIN HAVILAND. *Melville.* New York: Braziller, 1975. Psychobiography.

OLSON, CHARLES. *Call me Ishmael.* New York: Reynal & Hitchcock, 1947. *Moby-Dick* and Shakespeare.

PARKER, HERSHEL and HAYFORD, HARRISON, eds. *"Moby-Dick" as Doubloon: Essays and Extracts 1851–1970.* New York: Norton, 1970. Includes many reviews.

PERCIVAL, M. O. *A Reading of "Moby-Dick."* Chicago: University of Chicago Press, 1950. Interpretative monograph.

ROSENBERRY, EDWARD H. *Melville and the Comic Spirit.* Cambridge, Mass.: Harvard University Press, 1955. "The comic threads are as vital as the tragic ones to the rich suggestiveness" of *Moby-Dick.*

SALDÍVAR, RAMÓN. *Figural Language in the Novel: The Flowers of Speech from Cervantes to Joyce.* Princeton: Princeton University Press, 1984. Includes chapter on "The Apotheosis of Subjectivity: Performative and Constative in Melville's *Moby-Dick.*"

SEDGWICK, WILLIAM ELLERY. *Herman Melville: The Tragedy of Mind.* Cambridge, Mass.: Harvard University Press, 1945. Contains long chapter on *Moby-Dick.*

STANONICK, JANEZ. *"Moby-Dick": The Myth and the Symbol—A Study in Folklore and Literature.* Ljubljana, Yugoslavia: Ljubljana University Press, 1962.

STANZEL, FRANZ. *Narrative Situations in the Novel.* Translated by James P. Pusack. Bloomington: Indiana University Press, 1971. Includes discussion of the narratorial strategies in *Moby-Dick.*

STERN, MILTON R., ed. *Discussions of "Moby-Dick."* Boston: D.C. Heath, 1960. Reprints fifteen articles.

THOMPSON, LAWRENCE. *Melville's Quarrel with God.* Princeton: Princeton University Press, 1952. Christian doctrine and concepts are systematically ridiculed in *Moby-Dick*, which advocates heroic defiance of God's "infinite malice."

VINCENT, HOWARD P. *The Trying-Out of "Moby-Dick."* Boston: Houghton Mifflin, 1949. Reprint. Carbondale: Southern Illinois University Press, 1965. Reprint. Kent, Ohio: Kent State University Press, 1980. Exhaustive study of the cetological material.

WAY, BRIAN. *Herman Melville: "Moby-Dick."* Studies in English Literature series. London: Edward Arnold, 1977. Brief critical monograph.

ZOELLNER, ROBERT. *The Salt-Sea Mastodon: A Reading of "Moby-Dick."* Berkeley: University of California Press, 1973. "Learning to love *Leviathan,* the alien, the cosmic, other."

Articles

AUDEN, W. H. "The Christian Tragic Hero." *New York Times Book Review,* 16 December 1945, pp. 1, 21. Misreading of *Moby-Dick* as a Christian tragedy.

AUSBAND, STEPHEN. "The Whale and the Machine: An Approach to *Moby-Dick." American Literature* 47 (1975): 197–211.

BARBOUR, JAMES. "The Composition of *Moby-Dick*." *American Literature* 47 (1975): 343–60.

BAYM, NINA. "Melville's Quarrel with Fiction." *PMLA* 94 (1979): 909–23. Important discussion.

BELL, MILLICENT. "Pierre Bayle and *Moby-Dick*." *PMLA* 66 (1951): 626–48. Melville's use of Bayle's *Dictionnaire historique et critique*.

BLACK, STEPHEN A. "On Reading Psychoanalytically." *College English* 39 (1977): 267–74. Discusses the reader's engagement with the text of *Moby-Dick* from a psychoanalytical perspective.

CAMBON, GLAUCO. "Ishmael and the Problem of Formal Discontinuities in *Moby-Dick*." *Modern Language Notes* 76 (1961): 516–23. "Remembering spectator" replaces "remembered actor" as narrative focus.

CHARVAT, WILLIAM. "Melville and the Common Reader." *Studies in Bibliography* 12 (1959): 41–57.

GLENN, BARBARA. "Melville and the Sublime in *Moby-Dick*." *American Literature* 48 (1976): 165–82. The influence of Edmund Burke's *Philosophical Enquiry into the Origin of Our Ideas of the Sublime and Beautiful*.

HALVERSON, JOHN. "The Shadow in *Moby-Dick*." *American Quarterly* 15 (1963): 436–46. Jungian commentary.

HAYMAN, ALLEN. "The Real and the Original: Herman Melville's Theory of Prose Fiction." *Modern Fiction Studies* 8 (1962): 211–32.

HERBERT, T. WALTER, JR. "Homosexuality and Spiritual Aspiration in *Moby-Dick*." *Canadian Review of American Studies* 6 (1975): 50–58.

HOWARD, LEON. "Melville and the American Tragic Hero." In *Four Makers of the American Mind*, edited by Thomas Edward Crawley, pp. 65–82. Durham, N. C.: Duke University Press, 1976. Influence of Shakespearean tragedy and of Carlyle.

ISANI, MUKHTAR ALI. "Zoroastrianism and Fire Symbolism in *Moby-Dick*." *American Literature* 44 (1972): 385–97.

KOSOK, HEINZ. "Ishmael's Audience in 'The Town-Ho's Story'." *Notes and Queries* 14 (1967): 54–56. Reprinted in *"Moby-Dick" as Doubloon*.

LEE, A. ROBERT. "*Moby-Dick:* The Tale and the Telling." In *New Perspectives on Melville,* edited by Faith Pullin, pp. 86–127. Edinburgh: Edinburgh University Press, 1978.

LUCAS, THOMAS EDWARD. "Herman Melville: The Purpose of the Novel." *Texas Studies in Literature and Language* 13 (1972): 614–61. Summary of Melville's views on fiction.

MC INTOSH, JAMES. "Melville's Use and Abuse of Goethe: The Weaver-Gods in *Faust* and *Moby-Dick.*" *Amerikastudien/American Studies* 25 (1980): 158–73.

"*Melville Supplement,*" *Emerson Society Quarterly,* no. 28, part 3 (1962). Includes seven articles on *Moby-Dick,* several of which are on teaching the novel.

MIDLER, ROBERT. "The Composition of *Moby-Dick:* A Review and a Prospect." *Emerson Society Quarterly* 23 (1977): 203–16. Excellent analysis; largely supersedes Stewart's and Barbour's articles.

PAUL, SHERMAN. "Melville's 'The Town-Ho's Story'." *American Literature* 21 (1949): 212–21.

SEALTS, MERTON, J., JR. "Melville and Emerson's Rainbow." in *Pursuing Melville: Chapters and Essays 1940–1980,* pp. 250–77. Madison: University of Wisconsin Press, 1982. Thorough survey of a much discussed relation.

SHORT, R. W. "Melville as Symbolist." *University of Kansas City Review* 15 (1948): 38–46.

SHULMAN, ROBERT. "The Serious Function of Melville's Phallic Jokes." *American Literature* 33 (1961): 179–94. Beneath their surface, Melville's phallic jokes are characterized by hostility and defiance. The phallic imagery surrounding Moby Dick in the closing chapters helps to emphasize not creativity but primal, destructive force.

SMITH, HENRY NASH. "The Madness of Ahab." *Yale Review* 66 (1976): 14–32.

STEWART, GEORGE R. "The Two *Moby-Dick*s." *American Literature* 25 (1954): 417–48.

STOUT, JANIS. "Melville's Use of the Book of Job." *Nineteenth-Century Fiction* 25 (1970): 69–83.

VOGEL, DAN. "The Dramatic Chapters in *Moby-Dick.*" *Nineteenth-Century Fiction* 13 (1958): 239–47.

WARD, J. A. "The Function of the Cetological Chapters in *Moby-Dick.*" *American Literature* 28 (1956): 164–83.

WRIGHT, NATHALIA. "*Moby-Dick:* Jonah's or Job's Whale?" *American Literature* 37 (1965): 190–95.

ZIFF, LARZER. "Shakespeare and Melville's America." In *New Perspectives on Melville,* edited by Faith Pullin, pp. 54–67. Edinburgh: Edinburgh University Press, 1978.

Bibliographies

BEEBE, MAURICE, et al. "Criticism of Herman Melville: A Selected Checklist." *Modern Fiction Studies* 8 (1962): 312–46.

HIGGINS, BRIAN. *Herman Melville: An Annotated Bibliography.* Vol. 1, *1846–1930.* Boston: G. K. Hall, 1979.

PARKER, HERSHEL and HAYFORD, HARRISON. "An Annotated Bibliography." In *Moby-Dick as Doubloon: Essays and Extracts 1851–1970,* pp. 367–88. New York: Norton, 1970. *Moby-Dick* criticism from 1921 to 1969. For post-1969 listings see the bibliographies in *American Literature* and *PMLA.*

WRIGHT, NATHALIA. "Herman Melville." In *Eight American Authors: A Review of Research and Criticism,* edited by James Woodress, pp. 173–224. Rev. ed. New York: Norton, 1972.

Index

About the Author

Kerry McSweeney is the Molson Professor of English at McGill University in Montreal, where he teaches nineteenth-century British and American literature. His publications include *Tennyson and Swinburne as Romantic Naturalists, Four Contemporary Novelists,* and a book on George Eliot's *Middlemarch.* He has also edited *Diversity and Depth in Fiction: Selected Critical Writings of Angus Wilson.*